NORSE MAGICAL
AND HERBAL HEALING

A Medical Book from Medieval Iceland

NORSE MAGICAL
AND HERBAL HEALING

A Medical Book from Medieval Iceland

translated and edited by Ben Waggoner

© 2011
Troth Publications

DISCLAIMER: The information in this book is provided for the purposes of study only, and is not intended to treat, prevent, alleviate, or cure any disease. The efficacy of the measures described in this book has not been tested. Neither the author nor the publisher assume any liability for any effects resulting from following the measures described in this book. Persons with health concerns are urged to seek advice from licensed health care professionals.

A portion of this book was previously published in *IDUNNA*, no. 89 (2011).

Published by The Troth
24 Dixwell Avenue, Suite 124
New Haven, Connecticut 06511
http://www.thetroth.org/

ISBN-13: 978-0-578-09270-6

Troth logo designed by Kveldulf Gundarsson; drawn by 13 Labs, Chicago, Illinois

Cover design: Ben Waggoner

Typeset in Garamond 18/14/12

dedicated with love
to my wife, who knows
and passes on the knowledge

TABLE OF CONTENTS

INTRODUCTION

This book is a translation of one of the relatively few medical texts in Old Norse-Icelandic. Catalogued as AM 434a 12mo in the Arnamagnæan Institute at the University of Copenhagen, it was written around the year 1500. Though only 10.4 x 7.7 cm (about 4 inches x 3 inches), the manuscript is neatly written in two columns of text per page, in the handwriting of two different scribes. The text is missing its first pages, and its formal title, if it had one, is unknown.

AM 434a begins with a series of charms, spells, and prayers, both in Norse and in Latin of varying degrees of comprehensibility; some use Hebrew words or seeming nonsense syllables. The first charms and prayers are for healing purposes, but then comes a section of charms for decidedly non-therapeutic uses: winning at gambling, avoiding the hatred of enemies, catching thieves, and so on. There are magical symbols and inscriptions of various sorts. Following the charms is a brief set of health prognoses, and a *regimen*, a monthly list of measures to take to maintain one's health.

The bulk of the book—49 pages in the original—is a leechbook: a long list of complaints with remedies given for each one. In other books of this sort, the illnesses are organized "from head to toe", but here there seems to be no clear organization, although there is a tendency for remedies for the same or similar ailments to be grouped together. Following that is a "book of simples": an alphabetical list of ingredients, from *absinnthium* (wormwood) to *sal* (salt), with notes on how to use each one. Then comes a series of miscellaneous short texts: the uses of the steam-bath, a text on embryology, a poem on anatomy, an explanation of infertility, and two more charms. A *lunarium* follows, with prognostications for each day of the lunar cycle. Several "odds and ends" that probably belonged with the "book of simples", the charms, or the prognostics appear at the end.

AM 434a has received some attention from historians of magic, since some of its charms closely resemble charms and spells found in Icelandic grimoires, most of which date from the 17th and 18th centuries. The manuscript has also been studied by historians of medieval medicine. There has been relatively little attention paid to AM 434a in its entirety and in its context. To understand AM 434a in its entirety, and in its proper context, a brief review of the prehistory and history of medicine in northern Europe is in order.

PREHISTORY OF EUROPEAN HEALING TRADITIONS

In every culture, and for as far back in time as we have historical or archaeological evidence, humans have used plants to heal. Even chimpanzees and monkeys have been observed swallowing plants that are known to be effective against parasites and infections.[1] So it's likely that our not-fully-modern human ancestors did so, perhaps hundreds of thousands of years ago. In fact, the Neanderthal burials at Shanidar Cave, Iraq, 35,000–60,000 years old, included a grave with abundant remains of flowers, most of which have medicinal uses. The person in the grave has been hypothesized to have been a healer of some sort.[2] The origin of these flowers has been questioned—they may have been introduced by rodents, not deliberately buried[3]—but there is now direct evidence that Neanderthals at Shanidar and other sites gathered, cooked, and ate plant foods, making it quite plausible that they also used plants to treat illness.[4] Neanderthal burials and even older remains show evidence of congenital malformations and severe but healed injuries, suggesting that human ancestors took care of their sick and injured. [5] But regardless of who the very first herbalist was, the knowledge of which plants could cure or soothe which illnesses, and how to harvest and prepare them, must have been worked out through many centuries of trial and error and handed down orally, as it still is in many cultures.

The "fossil record" of healing by spiritual means—magic, religion, and the hazy borderlands between them—is much harder to interpret. Spoken prayers and spells leave no physical traces, except for written texts which only appear in relatively recent history and which have their own problems of interpretation. Objects used in magic, or depictions of magic rites and effects, are often extremely hard to interpret if we do not know the full cultural context. Nonetheless, artifacts such as the cave paintings of early modern *Homo sapiens* seem to have links with magic and ritual; some seem to show scenes from ritual itself. Artwork of this time has been linked to altered states of consciousness invoked as part of shamanistic practices.[6] If recent ethnography is any guide, it's likely that some of these practices were done to cure physical or spiritual sickness. In any case, the belief in healing the sick and defending the well by appeasing, requesting, or fighting unseen conscious powers seems to be as old as humanity and virtually universal among humans.

Plants for Healing

Conceptually, we tend to separate substances used to cure or alleviate bodily illnesses (medical drugs) from substances used for nutrition and taste enjoyment by healthy people (food) and substances used for their effects on the mind and perception (alcohol, narcotics, hallucinogens, and other drugs outside of the medical system, mostly illegal). However, many traditional peoples didn't, and don't, draw a distinction between these three uses. In many medical systems, and particularly in medieval European medicine, certain foods were prescribed for their healing effects, creating a continuous spectrum between "medicine" and "food". To give a familiar example: Chicken soup is clearly a food, and is often eaten by people in perfect health. At the same time, it's a common home remedy for colds and influenza, and it's often "prescribed" and used as a medicine would be used. Much the same could be said of the health foods, supplements, special diets, and "nutraceuticals" of today; they blur the distinction between food and medicine.

Psychoactive substances also overlap with both "food" and "medicine", creating continua instead of neatly defined categories. To give another familiar example: Coffee may be drunk for its flavor, as a home remedy for hangovers and headaches, or for the enjoyable caffeine "buzz." One person might drink coffee for any or all of these reasons at different times.

Some plants were originally cultivated for food and then came to be used medicinally; for others, medicinal use came first. Many psychoactive plants are thought to have been used first as foods, with their mental effects being discovered later. In many cases, it may be impossible to tell which came first.[7] Thus, for example, we know that the late Stone Age residents of what is now Zürich were growing lemon balm (*Melissa officinalis*). Whether they grew it to flavor their fish dishes, to cure their infections, or to calm their nerves is an unanswerable question, and probably a meaningless one. Quite possibly they used lemon balm for all these purposes, without recognizing any distinction between them; lemon balm was simply a plant that could be used in different ways, as needed. This is important to keep in mind when evaluating ethnobotanical or archaeological evidence. A great many plants had multiple uses, and any list of possible "medicinal plants" will overlap with lists of food plants and/or psychoactive plants. (To a lesser extent, all these lists will overlap with lists of dye plants and fiber plants; *Cannabis sativa*, for example, can be used for fiber, oil, or medicine— and as the current controversies over "medical marijuana" show, its medicinal, psychoactive, and even religious uses are rather tangled.) This point should be remembered while reading AM 434a and other medieval medical texts: plants that today are used almost exclusively for food, such as celery, mustard, parsnips, and radishes, are routinely called for in medicinal preparations. For that matter, simple foodstuffs such as honey, wine, eggs, broth, and even flour and bread have their medical uses as well.

A related problem is that a number of the plants listed in AM 434a are common weeds in fields and pastures. Plantain (*Plantago* spp.) and sorrel and dock (*Rumex* spp.) are probably the most widespread examples; it seems as if there is evidence for these in almost every site of archaeobotanical interest in Europe. While perhaps it stands to reason that prehistoric peoples would discover and use the most common plants in their environment for medicine, the simple presence of a common weed that has medicinal uses in folk biology does not mean that the ancient people knew or used that plant as medicine. Even evidence that such a "weed" was deliberately gathered may not be enough to show that it was used medicinally. This must also be kept in mind when evaluating data: there have been several claims made for ancient plants used deliberately, which may simply be fortuitous associations.[8]

Herbal Healing in Early Europe

Archaeology gives us a few glimpses of the use of medicinal plants in ancient Europe. For example, a number of sites in Germany and Switzerland, dated as far back as 5000-4500 BCE, have yielded cultivated poppy seeds (*Papaver somniferum*), although it's hard to say whether these were grown for use as a narcotic, or for their edible seeds.[9] A few late Stone Age sites from Germany, Switzerland, and elsewhere in Europe have yielded hemp seeds (*Cannabis sativa*). These could well have been grown for their oil or fiber, instead of (or in addition to) their psychoactive properties.[10] A late Neolithic burial at Ditfurt, Germany has yielded remains of plants that are likelier to have been used medicinally or ritually: henbane (*Hyoscyamus niger*), agrimony (*Agrimonia eupatoria*), hound's tongue (*Cynoglossum officinale*), and hemlock (*Conium maculatum*). Other Neolithic and later sites have yielded many remains of the ergot fungus (*Claviceps purpurea*), which produces compounds chemically similar to LSD—although whether ergot was deliberately used, in medicine or ritual, is not certain.[11] On perhaps a less sinister note, from about 3500 BCE on, people in what is now Switzerland also grew flavorful and possibly medicinal plants introduced from the Mediterranean, including dill (*Anethum graveolens*), celery (*Apium graveolens*), and lemon balm.[12]

These early Europeans also gathered wild plants, and archaeological sites contain their remains as well. Some of what they gathered could have been used as either food or medicine, such as wild roses, elderberries, bladder cherry (*Physalis alkekengi*), and parsley. Other plants that they used are not really edible, but are known to have medicinal properties, and probably fell towards the "medicine" end of the spectrum: for example, the Neolithic Seeberg site in Switzerland has yielded remains of bitter nightshade (*Solanum dulcamara*) and guelder rose (*Viburnum opulus*).[13] There have been claims that henbane was used at Neolithic sites in Scotland, presumably as a ritual hallucinogen, although reanalysis of the evidence has failed to support this conclusion.[14] However, the 7000-year-old Altscherbitz well in Germany has yielded sizable quantities of henbane seeds, together with both primary food plants such as wheat, barley and peas, and edible/medicinal plants such as rosehips.[15]

The famous "Ötzi the Ice Man", a mummified corpse frozen in a glacier on what is now the Austria-Italy border around 3300 BCE, was found carrying lumps of the birch fungus, *Piptoporus betulinus*. Although it's not certain why he had these, we do know that "Ötzi" suffered from intestinal roundworms—and *Piptoporus betulinus* does have laxative and anti-parasitic properties.[16]

Indo-European Medicine

The Germanic languages, along with most European languages, belong to a larger grouping known as Indo-European. The proto-language that gave rise to the Indo-European family of languages has been reconstructed as being spoken by people living on the Pontic-Caspian steppes, north of the Black Sea and Caspian Sea, between about 4500 and 2500 BCE. These people grew some grain but also practiced pastoralism, herding flocks of cows, sheep and goats; around 3700 BCE, one group of them domesticated horses. As these people began migrating into Europe around 3300 BCE, their language and culture were also adopted by other peoples who already lived there. This complex mixture of migration and cultural diffusion ultimately gave rise to the historic peoples who spoke Germanic languages, as well as speakers of Celtic, Italic, Baltic, Slavic, Greek, and other language groups.[17]

By comparing descendant languages, it is possible to reconstruct something of the language of the Proto-Indo-Europeans. While they had words for sickness in general (*suergh-*), texts in several Indo-European languages make a point of referring to sicknesses both "seen and unseen."[18] We can reconstruct specialized terms for outwardly visible illnesses, such as *dedrús*, "skin eruption"; *$h_1$elkes-*, "sore, ulcer"; *uolno-*, "wound"; *puh_1es*, "pus, infection"; *$h_2endhós$*, "blind"; and *$bhodh_xrós$*, "deaf".[19] On the other hand, we are unable to reconstruct specific words for internal diseases. The Proto-Indo-Europeans also had words for treatments: *h_1eis-*, "to refresh; to restore", gave rise to words for healing in several descendant languages, as did *iak(k)-*, "to cure," and *h_2eldh-*, "to achieve successfully." The root *med-* originally had the sense of "restoring a situation to normal by applying the correct measures"; it gave rise to Latin *medicus* and ultimately English "medicine," along with non-medical words such as "mediate" and "moderate".[20] Ideally, such treatments would make a sick person *koh_ailos*, "healthy, whole, complete". We can also reconstruct many anatomical terms, including not only words for virtually all of the external parts of the body, but words for internal organs, such as *kérd-*, "heart"; *$h_2eh_2(e)r-$*, "kidney"; *$iek^wr(t)$*, "liver; *$h_2óst$*, "bone"; and *$h_1ésh_2r$*, "blood".[21]

Comparative study of Indo-European texts and cultures suggests that the Proto-Indo-Europeans thought of medicine as consisting of three basic types: healing by magic spells, healing by surgery, and healing with plants and other medicines. These types align with the three major cultural "functions" that are typical of Indo-European cultures: rulership (subdivided into law and magic), war, and fertility. The three functions are reflected in everything from deities (gods of law and magic, war, and fertility) to social classes (rulers, warriors, and free farmers), and it seems that they appear in approaches to medicine as well.[22] Thus we can say that the Proto-Indo-Europeans knew the use of medicinal plants, and probably had specialists in their use. They may have had a myth telling how healing herbs appeared from the dismembered body of a sacrificed being: in Irish legend, healing plants came from the dismembered body of the healer Miacht, while in Iranian mythology, healing plants came from the body of a sacrificed ox. Several roots that we can reconstruct, such as *ghrei- and *h_3eng^w-, meant "to anoint" or "to rub on", and probably could refer to salves.[23] On the magico-religious side, we can reconstruct *keudes-, "magic force"; *alu-, "magic spell"; *meldh- and *g^whedh-, "to pray"; *gheu(h_x)-, "to invoke"; *spend-, "to make an offering, to perform a rite"; and so on.[24]

Amazingly, we can get some idea of what Indo-European healing charms, spells, and prayers were like. A 9th-10th-century Old High German charm for healing a wound, known as the Second Merseburg Charm, begins with a story of the god Balder's horse spraining its foot; the god Wodan and several goddesses are said to chant over it, and then the actual charm is given, including the words *ben zi bena, bluot zi bluoda, lid zi geliden, sose gelimida sin*—"bone to bone, blood to blood, limb to limb, so let them be joined." This charm has close parallels in several far-flung-Indo-European cultures: a Hittite document reads "Bone to bone is fitted, sinew to sinew is fitted, blood to blood is fitted," while an Irish legend includes the healing incantation "joint to joint of it, and sinew to sinew", and an Indian charm for healing a horse, from the *Atharva Veda*, includes the words "Let marrow be put together with marrow, let skin grow with skin; let your blood grow with blood, let flesh grow with flesh. . . Let your bone grow with bone."[25] This is evidence that the Proto-Indo-Europeans must have used a very similar charm, magically fitting together the separated parts of the injured limb from inside to outside.

Another 9th century charm, in Old Saxon, drives a "worm", possibly a literal parasite but perhaps a metaphor for infection, through concentric layers of the body: "Go out, worm, with your nine wormlings—out from the marrow to the bone; from the bone to the flesh; out from the flesh to the skin; out from the skin to the hoof!" This charm also has parallels in other Indo-European cultures and is likely to be extremely old.[26]

The Yamnaya culture, an Early Bronze Age group of probable Indo-European speakers living on the Pontic steppes north of the Black and Caspian seas, began to move into southeastern Europe by several routes, beginning around 3300 BCE. Their migration was once alleged to be a ferocious war of conquest, but the reality was much more complex and nuanced; while some fighting did occur, so did trading, patronage, intermarriage, and cultural diffusion, as Indo-European speakers mingled with the peoples already living in southern and eastern Europe.[27] We know little about their medicine or magic, but a Yamnaya grave from Gurbanesti, Romania has yielded carbonized hemp seeds, the oldest evidence for smoking hemp.[28] Over two thousand years later, the Greek historian Herodotus reported that the Scythians, an Indo-European people of the steppes, inhaled the smoke of burning hemp seed in purification rituals (and "howled in joy").[29] This particular use of hemp may well be an old Indo-European custom, introduced into Europe.

As Indo-European-speaking groups moved into Europe, they must also have been influenced in turn by the medicine and magic of the people who already lived there. Tracing this process is quite difficult now, but there may be some linguistic evidence. It has been argued that we can reconstruct a number of words in the northwestern European Indo-European languages that have no clear cognates in any other Indo-European languages. These may represent words that were borrowed by early Indo-European speakers from their neighbors. As Indo-European moved into northwestern Europe, its speakers probably adopted local names for plants that were new to them; the reconstructed words for "hazel", "willow", "rye", "hellebore", "cannabis", and "woad" seem to be unique to the northwestern European languages, and may have been borrowed from local languages.[30] By the time one branch of Indo-European had differentiated into what is now called Proto-Germanic, its speakers had adopted more words from their neighbors for a number of objects, including the words for the plants "clover", "dill", and "sweet gale"; these words can be reconstructed to Proto-Germanic, but do not seem to have wider Indo-European cognates.[31] This is a controversial topic, and some allegedly adopted words may turn out to be perfectly good Indo-European. Nonetheless, it's virtually certain that Indo-European concepts of healing, disease, herbs, and magic changed and expanded as they spread over most of Europe, as Indo-European speakers encountered new plants and possibly new diseases.

From the Bronze Age to the Roman Empire

Burials from the Bronze Age of Denmark, circa 1300 BCE, include remains of plants which could have been used in medicine and/or ritual. One female burial from Skrydstrup contained a sprig of wood chervil (*Anthriscus sylvestris*), and another, the famous "Egtved Girl," had been buried with a sprig of yarrow (*Achillea millefolium*).[32] Yet another Bronze Age burial from Denmark included a pouch containing dried roots and bark (species unfortunately not identified), animal bones, bird talons, small flint and bronze knives, a snake's tail, and other assorted objects. Such bags of odd items are fairly well-known from Bronze Age and later burials, and are usually interpreted as "medicine bags" used by physical or spiritual healers;[33] similar bags of miscellaneous small objects have been found in female Anglo-Saxon burials,[34] and bags of roots, bones, teeth, and other small objects used in curing are described in several early medieval accounts.[35] Finally, artistic motifs on rock carvings and metal artifacts provide possible evidence for the use of hallucinogenic *Amanita muscaria* mushrooms in Bronze Age Scandinavia.[36]

The late Stone Age and Bronze Age also provides us with early evidence of brewing mead and beer. Beer was invented in the Near East and probably entered Europe with the coming of agriculture; the oldest known traces of beer in Europe were found in Scotland, dating between 3000 and 1600 BCE.[37] These early beers often contained honey (making it rather arbitrary to classify them as "beer" or "mead"). They also usually contained herbs, some of which may have had psychoactive or physiological effects in addition to flavoring and/or preserving the beer. The early beers from Scotland contained meadowsweet (*Filipendula ulmaria*), henbane, heather (*Calluna vulgaris*), and royal fern (*Osmunda regalis*), while the Egtved Girl had beside her a bucket of wheat beer flavored with berries, honey, meadowsweet, and bog myrtle or sweet gale.[38] Bog myrtle continued to be used as a beer flavoring well into the Middle Ages, and in some parts of Norway as late as the mid-20th century; it added a sweet, fresh taste, but was "strongly intoxicating, with unpleasant after-effects" when drunk in large quantities.[39] The herb most commonly used to flavor beer today, hops (*Humulus lupulus*), may have been used in Norway as far back as the Stone Age, but not necessarily for brewing (the shoots are edible and the stems can be used for cordage); the oldest evidence for the use of hops in beer is from the 9th century or a little before.[40]

It has been alleged that the peoples of Northern Europe brewed herbal beers for both physical and psychotropic benefits, until the knowledge of brewing healing and enlightening beers was suppressed in favor of soporific, anti-aphrodisiac hopped beers.[41] This is difficult to demonstrate conclusively; most of the written evidence for brewing medicinal beers is post-medieval.[42] Nonetheless, even without herbs, beer (and wine and vinegar) are commonly prescribed in later medical texts, such as AM 434a, for making herbal infusions. Alcoholic drinks have also long been used medicinally for their intoxicating effects. There seems to be no reason why ancient beers with herbs could not have been used medicinally, in addition to their recreational, ritual, and social uses.

Later evidence for ancient diets and medicine in northwestern Europe comes from the famous Iron Age "bog people", sacrificed humans whose corpses have been amazingly well preserved by deposition in peat bogs. The stomachs of several "bog people" contained remains of gruel eaten shortly before their deaths, including both cultivated grains and wild seeds. One of the "bog people", a man from Grauballe, Denmark, had remains of over sixty different plant species in his stomach. These were primarily grains (emmer wheat, rye, barley, and oats) and weed seeds, some presumably harvested accidentally along with the grains, and others probably gathered for their nutritional value. This mixture was probably prepared as porridge or gruel; nutritious but not very appetizing, it may have been eaten only during hard times. Some researchers have considered the diverse nature of Grauballe Man's "last meal" to be ritually significant, but it seems to be a simple mixture of what was growing in the fields, prepared with sorting techniques that did not efficiently separate grains from weeds. There is no real evidence for the food being given with ritual or medicinal intent.[43] Grauballe Man also had eaten ergot fungus, which has psychoactive as well as medicinal properties; however, the amount he consumed does not seem to be high enough to have affected him much, and given that ergot is a common contaminant of grain, he may not have eaten them deliberately.[44] Yet his diet did include seeds of plantain, sorrel and dock, yarrow, and wild radish (*Raphanus raphanistrum*), which are also known from the diets of other "bog people."[45] Given that these are well documented in later manuscripts as medicinal, it would not be surprising if the "bog people" knew their medicinal uses, even though we cannot prove that that they did.

The first written documentation of the culture of Germanic-speaking peoples came from their neighbors the Romans, notably in the writings of Julius Caesar and Tacitus. Caesar claimed that the Germans were uninterested in agriculture, living primarily on meat, milk, and cheese.[46] Tacitus dismissed the Germans as indifferent farmers; they grew grain, but "although their land is fertile and extensive, they fail to take full advantage of it because they do not work sufficiently hard. They do not plant orchards, fence off meadows, or irrigate gardens".[47] Archaeology has proved both Caesar and Tacitus wrong. Pre-Roman sites in Germany and the Netherlands contain traces of small-scale plots that were probably garden sites, growing medicinal and/or culinary herbs such as catmint (*Nepeta cataria*), coriander (*Coriandrum sativum*), cumin (*Cuminum cyminum*), dill (*Anethum graveolens*), henbane, oregano (*Origanum vulgare*), parsley (*Petroselinum crispum*), and vervain (*Verbena officinalis*). Even in Sweden's somewhat colder climate, there is evidence for pre-Roman cultivation of celery (*Apium graveolens*), dill, henbane, and poppies, while a Roman-era site in Jutland, Denmark, yielded seeds of woad (*Isatis tinctoria*) and lingonberry (*Vaccinium vitis-idaea*), along with grains.[48]

That said, the Germanic peoples did learn some gardening from the Romans. Cabbage (*Brassica oleracea*), chicory (*Cichorium intybus*), cress (*Lepidium sativum*), mustard (*Brassica* sp.), parsnips (*Pastinaca sativa*), and rue (*Ruta graveolens*) appear for the first time in western Europe in the Roman period, although it's always possible that they were grown earlier and have not been found.[49] The Romans widely cultivated coriander, celery, dill, and summer savory (*Satureja hortensis*), while fennel (*Foeniculum vulgare*) and parsley are primarily found associated with Roman military bases, and caraway (*Carum carvi*) seems to have been popular along the German borders but not in the wider Empire.[50] The Romans also imported tropical herbs and spices into western Europe. We have direct archaeological evidence that the Romans imported cumin, sesame, and black pepper,[51] while written sources mention even more imported herbs and spices, such as ginger, mastic, and spikenard.[52]

Finally, Germanic-speaking people were exposed to Roman medicine by way of the Roman army, which built military hospitals along the frontier, concentrated along the Rhine and Danube. The hospital at Novaesium (now Neuss) on the Rhine was partially destroyed by fire in the 1ˢᵗ century AD, and the site has yielded a bundle of medicinal herbs preserved by carbonization, including henbane and centaury (*Centaurium umbellatum*). Other hospital sites have yielded surgical instruments and pots of ointment. We do not know whether such hospitals might have been open to non-soldiers, but in any case many Germanic-speaking people served in the legions and would have been exposed to Roman medicine. The legions' medical corps included many non-Roman doctors; possibly some Germans learned and practiced army medicine and introduced it to their own people after demobilization.[53]

By the end of the Empire, the peoples of Germany and Scandinavia were growing a great many domesticated plants which could have been used medicinally. A 4ᵗʰ-century site in south Germany shows that the inhabitants were growing celery, coriander, lemon balm, winter savory (*Satureja montana*), and an unknown species of *Allium* (onions, leeks, or garlic), while also gathering wild hops, elderberries, apples, pears, bramble berries, and other fruits.[54] Roman-era exotic imports largely disappear from the records with the collapse of the Empire, but pick up again in the Middle Ages as trade began to recover.

In the same time frame, the Germanic peoples began to use an alphabet known as the runes. Early rune inscriptions include many rather mundane inscriptions—personal names on burial stones and personal belongings, for example. Some, however, seem to have had a magical purpose—in particular the runes found on *bracteates*, thin round plates of gold with embossed designs that were probably carried as amulets. Apparent magic words on bracteates and other amulets include *alu* and *laukaz*. *Alu* is probably cognate with English "ale", but goes back to a Proto-Indo-European root that meant something like "magic spell". *Laukaz* is literally "leek", but in later Germanic writings, leeks are often used as symbols of vigorous growth, manliness, fertility, and offspring.[55] Bracteates and other early amulets also include wishes for good luck and good health, with words like *auja*, "good luck", *segun*, "blessing", and *bada* or *umbibada*, "protection."[56]

Plants were used medicinally by the Roman-era and post-Roman Germanic peoples, but they were also carried as amulets. A few Anglo-

Saxon burials include amulets of wood fibers or bark, or seeds worn as beads; others include small boxes that may have held herbs.[57] The laws of the Langobards prohibited a fighter in a trial by combat from carrying "witch's herbs" to give him an unfair advantage.[58] As late as the year 1000 CE, the German cleric Burchard of Worms condemned "evil phylacteries [protective amulets] using grass or amber" and "anything made of grass, or wood, or stone" tied to the body or sewn into clothing. Other pagan healing practices were documented by Christian clergy who opposed them. Gregory of Tours describes a heathen temple at Cologne, Germany, around the year 500, in which the locals made offerings, feasted, and, when in pain, carved wooden images of the affected body part.[59] This is of course a well-known practice from Greek temples of Asclepius. Other penitentials mention laying a child on a roof or in an oven to treat fevers,[60] or passing a child through a hole in the earth or in a stone, to cure or protect against illnesses.[61]

The Coming of Christianity

Beginning in the 4th century, the Germanic-speaking peoples living within the boundaries of the Roman Empire began to adopt Christianity, which by this time was the official religion of the Empire. As the Empire waned, the Church expanded its reach, and a long series of missionaries traveled into pagan regions to spread the gospel. The conversion process was sometimes peaceful and sometimes bloody; in Scandinavia, it ended with the last pagan king of Sweden, who by tradition is said to have died around 1080. While a king and his retainers might accept the new faith for a number of reasons—diplomatic alliances, trading rights, military threats, and so on—it took longer for the old ways to be suppressed among the commoners, and remnants of the old faith can be traced for several centuries after the nominal conversion of a region.

Christianity is sometimes seen as anti-intellectual, opposed to the enlightened knowledge of the pagan Greeks and Romans. This view is simply not true; while Christianity viewed some pagan learning as dangerous, it was Christian scholars and institutions that preserved most of what classical learning survived the collapse of the Roman Empire in the West.[62] Christian leaders attempted to suppress pre-Christian religions and traditions, and in some cases, Christians destroyed temples and holy places, even killing "sorcerors" and practitioners of the old ways. However, the Church soon found that suppressing the old ways entirely was neither possible nor desirable; the old ways and practices had filled real human needs. In order to attract people, the Church had to appropriate many of the old pagan practices for its own purposes, while taking care to avoid giving its approval to anything that might be genuinely heretical or otherwise dangerous.[63] So churches were built on the sites of pagan temples, feast-days of saints replaced pagan festivals, and miracle stories replaced pagan myths. Spells to restore health were functionally replaced by s; condemned pagan forms of divination were replaced by divinations using the Bible.[64] The pagan practice of tying herbs and amulets onto the body to cure disease was condemned by authors like St. Augustine; at the same time, Christians wore holy relics of saints on their bodies and attributed healing powers to them.[65] The 11th-century German priest Burchard of Worms condemned those who dug up medicinal herbs while speaking incantations—other than the *Credo* (the Creed) and *Pater Noster* (the Lord's Prayer), which were evidently allowable replacements for pagan magic spells.[66] Old pagan spells could be reused; the *Second Merseburg Charm* mentioned above has Christianized analogues all over Europe, in which Jesus, not Wodan, heals his wounded horse by saying "bone to bone, sinew to sinew" or something very similar.[67]

The line between pagan or heretical practices and acceptable ones was a fine one, and often a faint one. The Anglo-Saxon priest Ælfric, for example, strongly opposed divination, including divination by the moon. Yet he admitted that the moon seemed to have an effect on the earth and on living beings; animals and plants were stronger at the full moon than during a waning moon. To Ælfric, this was not *wiglung*, "divination," but *gecyndelic þing þurh gesceapenysse*, "a natural thing through creation."[68] Despite his denunciations, divinatory and prognostic texts based on the phases of the moon, and other natural phenomena such as lightning, circulated widely in the late Anglo-Saxon church.[69] Similarly, St. Augustine denounced the wearing of herbs and other objects as magical amulets, yet admitted that in some cases, wearing an object might be effective for unknown reasons. In such cases, what mattered was the intent of wearing the object. This loophole allowed Christians to wear various objects for protection, cures, and so on, in ways that differed little from the pagan use of amulets.[7]

Finally, aside from all its other effects, Christianity introduced the Germanic-speaking peoples to literacy and literature in Latin. The runes had never been used to record long texts; myths, poems, and traditional knowledge had been passed on orally. Literacy and the Latin alphabet, which was later adapted for most of the Germanic languages, made it possible to record some of the old lore, and also to read and write Latin texts, including medical manuscripts.

Christianity also brought monasticism northward, and with it the tradition of copying manuscripts. Monasticism also spread medical practices. Although some medieval monastics avoided medicine, or at least the learned medical traditions of ancient Greece and Rome, it came to be accepted that medical care, along with prayers and spiritual care, was worthwhile for monks to receive and to offer.[71] For example, St. Benedict approved of medical care in his *Rule*, allowing sick monks to have luxuries not allowed to well monks, such as meat and baths.[72] Monasteries also offered hospitality to pilgrims and travellers, and some provided medical care for needy lay persons.

Monasteries were intended to be self-sufficient communities with their own gardens,[73] and monastic medicine relied on herbs (as well as prayer and spiritual care). The *Plan of St. Gall*, a plan of an idealized monastery, called for a sizable infirmary, a separate room for bloodletting, a separate bathhouse, chapel, and kitchen for the sick, a kitchen garden, and a medicinal garden. The *Plan* listed lilies, roses, beans, summer savory, costmary (*Tanacetum balsamita*), fenugreek (*Trigonella foenum-graecum*), rosemary (*Rosmarinus officinalis*), mint, sage (*Salvia officinalis*), rue, iris, pennyroyal (*Mentha pulegium*), cress, cumin, lovage (*Levisticum officinale*), and fennel for the medicinal garden,[74] while the kitchen garden was to grow onions, leeks, garlic, shallots, celery, coriander, dill, poppy, radish, chard, parsley, chervil, lettuce, savory, parsnips, cabbage, and fennel.[75] Most of these could have been used in either cooking or medicine; because garden space was often limited, medieval gardeners tended to prefer plants with multiple uses.[76] Although the monastery depicted in the *Plan* was never actually built, the plants intended for its medicinal garden appear in many other sources for medieval gardening.[77] For example, the monk Walafrid Strabo wrote a poem about his own garden, *De Cultura Hortorum*, also known as *Hortulus*; he listed twenty-four plants and gave medicinal uses for most of them, beginning with sage and rue, and including wormwood (*Artemisia absinthium*), horehound (*Marrubium vulgare*), fennel, lovage, mint, pennyroyal, celery, betony (*Stachys officinalis*), agrimony, and radish.[78] When plants or texts were not available locally, monks and priests exchanged medical books, herbs, seeds, and advice.[79] As trade with the Indies recovered, wealthy monasteries also purchased exotic spices for use in medicine, including cinnamon, ginger, pepper, and galangal.[80]

Outside of the monasteries, Charlemagne's *Capitulare de Villis*, a detailed set of orders for how the royal estates were to be run, lists no fewer than ninety-five plant varieties that were expected to be grown.[81] Records from two of Charlemagne's villas show that the actual numbers were more modest. Some of the plants named in *Capitulare de Villis* are Mediterranean plants that would not have grown well in northern Europe; these may have been copied from classical sources but not actually grown. Still, the list includes well-known plants such as sage, rue, dill, celery, cumin, fennel, garlic, onions, lovage, mint, and pennyroyal.[82] Like monasteries, secular rulers bought and exchanged medicines from distant lands; to give one famous example, Elias the Patriarch of Jerusalem sent some exotic remedies and instructions for their use to King Ælfred of Wessex in the late 9th century.[83]

Medieval European medical practice was transformed once again by the rediscovery of Greek and Roman authorities whose works had been translated, expanded, and commented on by scholars in the Islamic Caliphate. Arabic scholars in the 9th century translated most of the works of Hippocrates, Galen, and other authorities into Arabic. Later authorities such as Avicenna (Ibn Sina), Rhazes (al-Razi), and Abulcasis (Abu al-Qasim) wrote their own books, expanding on the Greek medical tradition and bringing their own extensive experience to bear. This tremendous body of knowledge began filtering back into Europe in the 11th and 12th centuries, spurred by the work of translators such as Constantine Africanus and Gerard of Cremona.[84]

As early as the 10th century, the city of Salerno, Italy was a center for medical instruction. Legend has it that the "school" of Salerno was founded by four doctors: a Roman, a Greek, a Muslim, and a Jew. While this is not historical, it captures the eclectic nature of the medical education at Salerno, which drew heavily on the newly discovered and translated texts of Greco-Roman and Islamic medicine.[85] "Salernitan" medicine spread rapidly all over Europe—as far as Iceland, in fact. By about 1155, Nikulás, an Icelandic abbot who wrote a guidebook for pilgrims to the Holy Land based on his own experiences, mentioned "Salerniborg," *þar ero læknar beztir*—"where the best healers are."[86]

MEDIEVAL SCANDINAVIAN MEDICINE

Except for basic first aid and over-the-counter drugs, we tend to think of medicine as something practiced only by highly trained specialists. But in medieval Europe in general, academically trained physicians were virtually nonexistent before the 12th century. Even afterwards, they were rare, and available only to the wealthy. Medieval medicine has been compared to carpentry today: most people can do simple home repairs; some have a reputation as "handymen" and may be called on by friends and neighbors; relatively few take classes or undergo an apprenticeship in the building trades; and very few take the long, formal, theoretical training to become engineers or architects. In the same way, most medieval adults would have known some "home remedies" for common ailments; a few people in each district or village might have a reputation for skill in midwifery or herbalism or bone-setting or magical healing; even fewer people might study medicine under expert instruction; and only a tiny elite ever studied at a university.[87]

We see this pattern in the "sagas of Icelanders" and "contemporary sagas", prose narratives which are set in Iceland, more or less between the first Norse settlement around 870, and the absorption of Iceland into Norway in 1263. Family members took care of each other's wounds and sicknesses, but a person who gained a reputation as *góðr læknir*, "a good healer", might be sought out by sick or injured people outside his or her own household.[88] Other healers got on-the-job training, or learned healing within their own families, if we can believe the account in *Magnúss saga ins Góða*: Faced with a shortage of healers after a battle, King Magnús ordered the twelve men with the softest hands to bandage wounds. All twelve men went on to become excellent healers, despite having no previous experience; two of them were Icelanders, whose descendants also became renowned as healers.[89] A very few Norsemen went to Europe for medical study—Hrafn Sveinbjarnarson (d. 1213), a descendant of one of King Magnús's wound-dressers, traveled extensively in Europe and learned Salernitan medicine and surgery.[90] Bits and pieces of Salernitan medical texts turn up embedded in sagas, law codes, and other old manuscripts, and several sagas describe surgical techniques that are recognizably Salernitan. Icelanders and other Scandinavians who studied theology in Europe, as well as foreign monks and priests who visited or stayed in Scandinavia, may have had varying amounts of medical training, or brought medical books with them. Norsemen serving in the Varangian Guard in Byzantium, making pilgrimages to Rome, or crusading in the Middle East may also have picked up medical knowledge.[91] Medieval Norwegian law codes laid out healers' legal responsibilities, and one of them defines "lawful healers" as those who could treat major wounds; while these do not necessarily refer to university-trained physicians, they do seem to indicate increasing recognition of well-trained healers as a special class.[92]

We have direct archaeological evidence for plant cultivation and herbal medicine in the Viking era. Excavations at the Viking-era settlements in present-day York, England have revealed what may be the most direct evidence for the medicinal use of herbs: The material filling a waste or latrine pit from the mid- to late 9th century included seeds of caper spurge (*Euphorbia lathyris*) and white bryony (*Bryonia cretica dioica*), along with fragments of bran and other remains of digested food. These herbs would not have been part of the regular diet, as they have strong purgative effects, but they would have been effective against intestinal worms—and the latrine pits from York contain abundant eggs of both whipworm (*Trichuris*) and giant worm (*Ascaris*), showing that intestinal parasites were fairly widespread in the population.[93] Many other plants from York could have been used in both cooking and medicine. Celery, dill, leeks (*Allium porrum*), coriander, summer savory, hops, parsnips, carrots (*Daucus carota*), sweet gale (*Myrica gale*), and poppies have all been documented from York, as have rarer remains of fennel and black mustard (*Brassica nigra*). Potentially medicinal fruits from York include rose hips and elderberries, alongside apples and bramble fruits. There is little evidence for household gardens at York, but many "weeds" grew there that could have been used medicinally: nettle, sorrel, plantain, vervain, celandine (*Chelidonium majus*), horehound, catmint, henbane, and agrimony.[94]

Viking-era sites in Denmark have yielded remains of the probable medicinal herbs ground elder (*Aegopodium podagraria*) and celandine; potentially medicinal "weeds" such as sorrel, mugwort, and cornflower (*Centaurea cyanus*); and multi-use plants such as coriander, elder, hops, and sweet gale. A female grave at Fyrkat contained hundreds of henbane seeds, which had probably been in a small pouch; it's possible that the woman in the grave was a healer, or, given henbane's psychoactive properties, a magical practitioner of some sort.[95] Henbane is well documented from Viking and post-Viking-era Finland, as well as at other sites in Scandinavia.[96] From the 9th-century Viking site of Kaupang, Norway, we have evidence of wild roses, blackberries, apples, hops, and the usual "weeds" including henbane, plantain, yarrow, sorrel, and dock.[97] The Oseberg ship burial, dated to around the year 850, contained the body of a high-status woman buried with a wide range of grave goods; besides kitchen and farm equipment and rich textiles, the woman was laid to rest with a bucket of wild apples, some hazelnuts and grains, an imported walnut, a few seeds of flax and hemp, a box of woad fruits, and a box of cress seeds.[98] In Sweden, Viking-age Birka has yielded remains of meadowsweet, hops, plantain, nettles, sorrel, and mints,[99] while Viking-age Staraja Ladoga adds a few probably cultivated herbs such as marjoram (*Origanum vulgare*), motherwort (*Leonurus cardiaca*), and the ubiquitous henbane.[100]

Medieval Norwegian monasteries followed the same traditions as monasteries elsewhere in Europe, providing medical care and growing medicinal gardens, as well as kitchen gardens and orchards. Medicinal plants that still grow at monastery sites, and that were probably introduced by the monks, include sweet flag (*Acorus calamus*), bugloss (*Anchusa officinalis*), bryony (*Bryonia alba*), catmint, celandine, elder, henbane, hound's tongue, hyssop (*Hyssopus officinalis*), lovage, motherwort, valerian (*Valeriana officinalis*), and wormwood, to name a few. Norwegian monasteries also grew dual-use plants such as fennel, parsnips, coriander, caraway, and opium poppy.[101]

Iceland has relatively few native plants, partly because of its harsh climate and partly because of repeated volcanic eruptions. Beginning around the year 870, settlers in Iceland introduced plants from Britain and/or Scandinavia to Iceland, whether deliberately or accidentally. Fossil pollen found in bog sediments shows that valerian, plantain, and *Artemisia* (wormwood, mugwort, or another species) all appeared in Iceland soon after human settlement.[102] Also noteworthy is a pre-Christian female grave at Ytra-Garðshorn; the woman had been buried with a piece of beeswax, fifty-eight quartz crystals, and a pair of tweezers, probably all carried in a pouch. The woman may well have been a healer: the wax, which must have been imported as bees are not native to Iceland, could have been used in making salves (although any herbs she might have carried with her have apparently not survived), the tweezers for minor surgery, and the quartz stones in magical healing.[103] The Ytra-Garðshorn woman's sex is not surprising; the "sagas of Icelanders" list a number of women who were considered healers (*læknir*) and who treated severe battle injuries.[104]

Pre-Christian Scandinavian religion and mythology had a role for divine healing. In a prayer contained the poem *Sigrdrífumál*, the gods and goddesses are asked for *læknishendr, meðan lifum*—"healer's hands, while we live." The main summary of the mythology, Snorri Sturluson's *Edda*, mentions a goddess named Eir who is said to be "the best of healers."[105] Unfortunately, little more is known about her, and there is no evidence that she was widely worshipped.[106] Other mythological texts depict the god Óðinn as having great healing skill.[107] Outside Scandinavia, both Old English and Old High German healing charms name Woden or Wodan, the counterpart of Óðinn; in the Old English *Nine Herbs Charm*, Woden is said to have taken nine "glory-twigs" and struck and killed a snake that personifies disease. The "glory-twigs" are implied to be the nine healing plants listed in the charm; though some of the names are hard to interpret, a reasonable interpretation is that they are mugwort, plantain, cress, nettle, betony, chamomile, crab apple, chervil, and fennel.[108]

There are scattered references in the Eddas and sagas to various healing techniques. The best-known example appears in a poem called *Hávamál*—"The Speech of the High One", presented as the words of Óðinn himself—in the compilation known as the *Poetic Edda*. Verse 137, part of which appears to have been inserted from another source, lists a number of remedies:

> *Ráðumk þér, Loddfáfnir,   en þú ráð nemir, -*
> *njóta mundu, ef þú nemr,*
> *þér munu góð, ef þú getr -:*
> *hvars þú öl drekkir,   kjós þér jarðar megin,*
> *því at jörð tekr við ölðri,   en eldr við sóttum,*
> *eik við abbindi,   ax við fjölkynngi,*
> *höll við hýrógi,   - heiftum skal mána kveðja, -*
> *beiti við bitsóttum,   en við bölvi rúnar,*
> *fold skal við flóði taka.[109]*

I advise you, Loddfafnir,   that you take this advice,—
    you will benefit from it, if you take it,
    it will be good for you, if you get it—:
when you drink ale,   choose earth's power for yourself,
because earth counters drinking,   but fire against illnesses,
oak against constipation,   an ear of grain against sorcery,
ergotized rye against a wound,   —you must invoke the moon
    for hatred,—
earthworms against illness from animal bites,   but runes
    against evil,
    earth shall counter a flood.

The text is not perfectly clear—höll við hýrógi could mean either "elder-tree against unrest at home" or "ergot-infected rye against a wound", and beiti could be "earthworms", "heather", or "alum", depending on which scholar you believe.[110] Nonetheless, this is evidence for healing techniques known in Iceland around the time of the Christian conversion.

Verses from Sigrdrífumál (5, 8, 9, 11) also refer to healing or preserving health using both plants and magic:

Bjór færi ek þér,   brynþings apaldr,
magni blandinn   ok megintíri;
fullr er hann ljóða   ok líknstafa,
góðra galdra   ok gamanrúna.

Full skal signa   ok við fári sjá
        ok verpa lauki í lög;
þá ek þat veit,   at þér verðr aldri
        meinblandinn mjöðr.

Bjargrúnar skaltu kunna,   ef þú bjarga vilt
        ok leysa kind frá konum;
á lófum þær skal rísta   ok of liðu spenna
        ok biðja þá dísir duga.

Limrúnar skaltu kunna,   af þú vilt læknir vera,
        ok kunna sár at sjá;

á berki skal þær rísta   ok á baðmi viðar,
        þeim er lúta austr limar.

Beer I bring to you,   apple-tree of the mailcoat-assembly,[111]
blended with strength   and glory from power;
it is full of songs   and healing staves,
good magic spells   and runes of pleasure.

You shall bless a cup   and beware of harm,
        and throw a leek in the drink;
then I know   that mead will never be
        blended with harm for you.

Saving-runes shall you know,   if you want to save
        and release children from mothers;
on the palms you shall carve them   and clasp the joints
        and ask the female spirits to help.

Limb-runes shall you know,   if you want to be a healer,
        and know how to look after wounds;
on bark you shall carve them   and on branches of trees,
        on those which bow their limbs eastwards.

One other poem in the *Edda*, *Oddrúnarkviða*, describes the healer Oddrún using magic spells to help in a difficult childbirth: *ríkt gól Oddrún, rammt gól Oddrún, bitra galdra at Borgnýju*—"Oddrun powerfully chanted, Oddrún strongly chanted, bitter spells for Borgný." This is similar to the "saving-runes" in *Sigrdrífumál*, and there is no reason why these passages could not refer to actual practice.

The prose "sagas of Icelanders" include instances of runes used for healing. In the best-known, an episode in *Egils saga skallagrimssonar*, a farmer's son falls in love with a girl and carves runes on a stick, slipping the stick into her bed to make her love him. However, he makes a mistake in his carving, and the girl falls ill. The hero of the saga, Egil Skallagrimsson, finds the stick, scrapes off the runes, and carves new ones on; when he places this next to the girl, she instantly recovers. Egil says:

Skalat maðr rúnar rísta,
nema ráða vel kunni.
Þat verðr mörgum manni,
es of myrkvan staf villisk.
Sák á telgðu talkni
tíu launstafi ristna.
Þat hefr lauka lindi
langs ofrtrega fengit.

A man must not carve runes
unless he knows well how to interpret them.
It happens to many men
that the dark stave goes wrong.
I saw on the hewn whalebone
ten secret letters carved.
That has brought long suffering
to the linden-of-leeks.

We can compare accounts like this one to archaeological evidence of rune-inscribed amulets made to either heal the bearer, or to defend him or her against illness. The earliest dates from around the year 725: a piece of human skull from Ribe, Denmark, is carved with two lines of runes that invoke "Ulf and Odin and High-Tyr" against "pain and dwarf-stroke".[112] A later amulet, an 11th-century copper plate from Sigtuna, Sweden, addresses the disease itself as an "ogre" (*þurs*) and a "wolf":

Ogre of wound-fever, lord of the ogres! Flee now! You are found.
Have for yourself three pangs, wolf!
Have for yourself nine needs, wolf!
iii ice [runes]. These ice [runes] may grant that you be satisfied, wolf.
Make good use of the healing charm![113]

Yet another amulet from Sigtuna, carved on a bone and dated to the 11th or 12th century, has not been fully interpreted but includes the lines "He bound the fever, he fought the fever and fucked the sorcerer."[114] Rune amulets for healing and protection continued to be made well after the coming of Christianity, sometimes combining pagan and Christian imagery; one inscription on a wooden wand from Ribe, Denmark, dated to 1300, reads in part:

> I pray earth to guard   and high heaven
> the sun and holy Mary   and the lord God himself,
> that he grant me   leech-hands [i.e. healing hands]
> and a healing tongue   to heal the trembler
> when a cure is needed.
> From back and from breast,   from body and from limbs,
> from eyes and from ears;   from wherever evil can enter.[115]

The invocation to "earth and high heaven" has many parallels in Norse and other Germanic languages, and the prayer for healing hands and a healing tongue is much like the request that the gods grant "healing hands" in *Sigrdrífumál*. Another amulet from Bergen, Norway, dated to 1335, appears to be a love-charm but begins with a statement of protection from harmful disease-causing spirits: "I cut cure-runes (*bótrúnar*), I cut help-runes (*bjarg-rúnar*); once against the elves, twice against the trolls, thrice against the ogres. . ."[116] Yet another amulet from Bergen, Norway, from the late 14th or early 15th century, bears a Latin inscription in runes, which reads in part:

> May God's five wounds be my medicine.
> May my medicine be the holy Cross and Christ's passion.
> He who molded and washed me with holy blood,
> expelled the fever which strove to torment me.[117]

The "sagas of Icelanders" have fewer references to herbs, but some Icelanders did grow gardens: *Laxdæla saga* mentions Guðrún Ósvifsdóttir's *laukagarðr* or "leek-yard", presumably a kitchen garden that may have grown other herbs as well.[118] A few other literary texts mention a *laukagarðr*, as do several old Norwegian law codes that lay out penalties for the theft of produce.[119] One of the few native edible plants of Iceland, angelica (*Angelica archangelica*, or *hvönn* in Norse), is also mentioned in the sagas; *Fóstbræðra saga* describes two brothers gathering angelica on a cliff,[120] while *Óláfs saga Tryggvasonar* mentions angelica stalks sold in a market.[121] Angelica was often gathered wild; the earliest written legal code for Iceland, *Grágás*, mentions penalties for gathering it on another person's lands. Some of the early Norwegian law codes mention private angelica gardens, as well as leek gardens.[122] Aside from being eaten, herbs could also be carried as amulets: in *Kormáks saga*, Steinarr brags that he's never needed to "bind a bag to my neck, full of herbs."[123]

But the best-known use of herbs in healing comes from an account of the aftermath of the battle of Stiklastad, which appears in several sagas. A healer is shown treating the wounded, cleaning their wounds with warm water; in *Fóstbræðra saga*, their wounds are said to be so severe that a groaning sound is coming from the wounds themselves. In one version of this saga, the healer offers the wounded hero Thormod some milk, which she says "gives strength to the wounded." She is also shown boiling up leeks and other herbs into a porridge, and feeding it to the wounded. This allows her to diagnose how critical the wound is; a wound that has pierced all the way to the guts will smell of leeks.[124] Assuming the saga account describes what an actual healer would do, and given the fairly frequent medicinal use of leeks (not always distinguished from garlic, onions, etc.) in AM 434a and other medical manuscripts, it's quite possible that the porridge was intended to have a direct healing effect as well as a diagnostic use. (One wonders what the other herbs in the porridge were.)

The legendary Norse sagas, or *fornaldarsögur*, mention plants with healing and magical properties more frequently than the more realistic *Íslendingasögur*. *Ragnars saga loðbrókar* mentions a *vínlaukr* or "wine-leek", which can keep a person alive for a long time with no other food.[125] *Völsunga saga* describes an herb that Sigurðr uses to heal the terrible wound that he has inflicted to the throat of his son Sinfjötli,[126] and *Hálfdanar saga Brönufóstra* describes herbs that the hero places under the heroine's pillow to make her fall in love with him.[127] Other sagas describe potions that can cause or cure illnesses such as leprosy.[128] Several texts mention lost body parts being preserved alive by being covered with herbs: a god's head,[129] a horse phallus,[130] a severed hand,[131] and amputated feet.[132] A text written about 1250, the *King's Mirror*, mentions a legendary floating island in an Irish lake, where healing herbs grew, along with a willow tree that miraculously bore apples that would heal whomever ate them.[133] While few if any of these accounts have a basis in fact, they do show that Icelanders were quite familiar with the idea of healing plants.

Iceland officially adopted Christianity in the year 1000. As it had everywhere else, Christianity brought access to Latin literacy and to the surviving medical literature. Monasteries were founded in Iceland, beginning with the monastery at Thingeyrar in 1133. As usual, they offered medical care for monks and lay persons, and the monks cultivated medicinal plants. Traveling clerics probably brought seeds and bulbs with them, or brought supplies of dried herbs to places where they could not be grown. While Iceland's climate made it difficult or impossible to grow many herbs, there are records of a *laukagarðr* at the church at Hólar in the 15th and 16th centuries, and probably well before.[134] Archaeologists have found evidence of sweet gale, yarrow, burnet, tansy (*Tanacetum vulgare*), and caraway at Icelandic monasteries;[135] one medicinal plant, butterbur (*Petasites hybridus*), still grows near monastic sites in Norway, Denmark, and Iceland, suggesting that it was introduced to Iceland for medicinal use.[136] A marginal note in the Royal Irish Academy manuscript 23 D 43 mentions that the medicinal plant *Baldurs-brá*, "Balder's brow", grew at the monastic site of Skriða in Hörgárdalur.[137] In all likelihood, Scandinavian and Icelandic monasteries bought and traded medicines that could not be grown or found locally, just like monasteries in Britain and the Continent. In order to celebrate the liturgy correctly, Scandinavian and Icelandic churches and monasteries had to be regularly supplied with wine, oil, and incense, which all had medicinal uses; perhaps stores of herbs were acquired by the same channels.

The last monastery founded in Iceland, Skriðuklaustur, was established in 1493, at about the time that AM 434a was written, and seems to have functioned as a center for medical treatment. Skeletons buried in the cemetery show a wide range of pathologies; surgical lancets were unearthed at the site; and pollen analysis reveals that medicinal plants were grown in the garden, including at least three that are not native to Iceland (plantain, nettle, and a species of *Allium*).[138] AM 434a may not have been written at Skriðuklaustur, and it may not have been written for monastic use—a similar book, MS D 23 43, was written for a secular leader.[139] Yet AM 434a probably gives a good idea of the level of care and the resources available at Skriðuklaustur.

Thus the compiler of AM 434a had a deep heritage to draw on. On the one hand, some of his herbal recipes could have roots going back to the Stone Age. On the other hand, he was working late enough that he could have been influenced by the printed medical books that were just beginning to circulate in northern Europe.[140] The richness of this historical heritage explains how the same magic charm can invoke the pagan deities Frigg and Freyja, Thor and Odin, right alongside Jesus Christ, Enoch, Elijah, and the Virgin Mary. It explains how runes and runelike symbols can mingle with garbled Hebrew words and letters. It explains how prescriptions for exotic spices from the East Indies could sit next to prescriptions for common Scandinavian weeds, and how an extract from a late Roman medical authority could be included alongside an Old Norse poem in traditional meter.

Norse Medical Manuscripts

AM 434a contains many parallels to three other major Icelandic medical texts. One fragment, written between 1250 and 1300, is now catalogued as AM 655 XXX; it is a list of complaints, each with one or more remedies usually containing herbs. The central "leechbook" section of AM 434a includes virtually all of the text of AM 655 XXX with only minor differences; the two even share some textual errors. The leechbook section of AM 434a could well have been copied from AM 655 XXX itself when it was complete, or else from a closely related manuscript.

The manuscript AM 194 is a compendium of short texts on medicine, geography, history, and similar topics. A reference in the text dates the book to the year 1387. The section of AM 194 known as *Læknisfræði* (*Medical Knowledge*) is largely contained in AM 434a, although the ordering of the material is different. AM 194 also contains a brief text on human embryology, *Myndan mannslíkama* (*The Form of the Human Body*), which closely parallels a passage in AM 434a.

Finally, the Royal Irish Academy manuscript MS 23 D 43, translated and published in 1931, is the largest surviving medical manuscript in Norse. Like AM 434a, it begins with a section of charms and prayers, some of which resemble those in AM 434a. It contains a "book of simples" containing all the entries found in AM 434a and many more. It also contains a leechbook with many entries in common with AM 434a. However, the order and organization of entries in the leechbook is very different from AM 434a; the compiler, or one of his sources, apparently tried to group entries for the same illness together, and arrange the entries into "head to feet" order, although he did not complete this.[141] MS 23 D 43 also contains a translation of a book of compound medicines known as the *Antidotarium Nicolai*; a short lapidary (text on the properties of stones and gems); and a cookbook.

The best-known medieval Scandinavian medical authority is Henrik Harpestræng, a Danish priest who died in 1241. Harpestræng is noted for introducing Salernitan medical concepts into Scandinavia; although he was not the only Scandinavian to study Salernitan medicine, he was the first whose writings have been preserved. Most of Harpestræng's writings are translated or derived from works by Salernitan authors, notably *De viribus herbarum* by Odo Magdunensis and *De gradibus liber* by Constantine Africanus.[142] The *Antidotarium Nicolai* found in MS 23 D 43 is another Salernitan text, although Harpestræng himself may not have known it; there were several routes by which Salernitan books and concepts could have spread to Scandinavia.

Parts of AM 434a are paralleled in Harpestræng's known writings, notably the section dealing with simples, which is essentially an abridged Norse translation of Harpestræng's work. AM 194 also contains some material from Harpestræng, including a version of the book of simples; MS 23 D 43 includes a very complete version of Harpestræng's book of simples. AM 434a and AM 194 differ enough from each other in what material is included that they represent independent reworkings of Harpestræng's writings. AM 655 XXX, however, is not based on Harpestræng's work,[143] although it contains medical advice compiled from various sources, some of which could have been Harpestræng's writings or his sources.[144]

There are also parallels between AM 434a and Anglo-Saxon texts. The prognostics in AM 434a, such as the lunarium and the regimen, could have come from anywhere in western Europe, but some of them seem to resemble Old English material most closely. AM 434a cites the Anglo-Saxon scholar Bede as an authority; both AM 434a and MS 23 D 43 contain sections copied from Bede, or at least from texts attributed to Bede.

Given these likely Anglo-Saxon links, it's interesting to compare the medical recipes and "simples" of AM 434a with Anglo-Saxon medical texts. Anglo-Saxon recipes are likely to call for mixtures of many herbs, prepared in elaborate ways. To give just one example, this is a recipe from AM 434a, also found in AM 665 XXX:

> For an ache in the eyes, take the root of the herb called vervain and leaves of the herb called fennel and grind them both together and place them in the eyes..

Compare that with an Old English recipe from the *Lacnunga*:

> As an eye-salve: take aloes and zedoary, laurel berries and pepper; slice small, and lay fresh cow['s milk] butter on water; then take a broad whetstone and rub the butter on the whetstone with copper so that it be very stiff and then add some part of the plants to it; smear it then into a bronze vessel, let it stand nine nights and let it be turned each day, then let it be melted in the same bronze vessel; strain it out through a cloth; then put it into whichever vessel you want to; use then when it be needful; this salve has power against all kinds of infirmities which ail the eyes.[145]

And that's not the most complex recipe in *Lacnunga*. One recipe for a headache salve calls for no fewer than forty-six different plants, plus fat from five animals, marrow from two animals, bones, wine, wax, incense, and soap![146] Other Anglo-Saxon recipes include ritual actions to perform, and many include spells to recite—whether half-pagan charms, Christian prayers, or gibberish. The Norse recipes are generally much simpler; they rarely call for more than two or three ingredients, or for any actions other than simply preparing and taking the medicine. That said, some of the recipes in AM 434a and the Anglo-Saxon manuscripts do seem to share a common tradition; while the wording is rarely parallel, sometimes the ingredients of recipes are similar, such as the use of ink and sulfur together in both AM 434a and *Bald's Leechbook*.

Still more material was added to these medical texts as they circulated from Denmark through Norway, and from there to Iceland.[147] The time in which they were compiled was the time in which the Scandinavian languages were drifting apart, and analysis of the vocabulary shows a number of words derived from Old Danish, with a second "layer" of vocabulary derived from Old Norwegian. Shaun Hughes points out that

German medical texts were circulating in Scandinavia during the time of the Hanseatic League, and these were probably also incorporated into Norse writings.[148] On the other hand, some of the remedies in AM 434a, such as the use of dock (*Rumex* sp.), were used in the North well before continental texts were introduced.[149] AM 434a is thus a complex mixture of "native" and "learned" healing traditions, drawn together from different nations and regions of Europe.

AM 434a has also left "descendants" as well as ancestors, especially concerning its magical charms. Icelandic folklore contains many stories of magicians—usually clergy—who knew magic very well and owned magic books; although the best of them used their powers only for good, they still bore a rather sulfurous reputation for alleged dealings with devils and such.[150] Iceland saw a number of witch trials between 1554 and 1720; almost all of the accused were men, most were not executed, and almost half of them included accusations of using magical signs and symbols.[151] Records exist, sometimes fairly detailed, of books of magic that were condemned and destroyed. The oldest surviving book of magic, the *Galdrabók*, was compiled by several hands between 1550 and 1680.[152] The tradition of writing magic books survived well into the 19th century, and a number of later manuscripts have been preserved.[153] Their contents include identical or very similar charms and signs to AM 434a, with a very similar mixture of Latin, Hebrew, and unidentifiable words and phrases, and a similar mixture of Christian prayers and invocations with a dash of Germanic paganism. Some of these signs, such as the *Ægishjálmr* or "Helm of Awe", are mentioned in earlier texts such as the *Poetic Edda*, but AM 434a is the oldest depiction of them. As such, AM 434a is the oldest documentation of the Icelandic grimoire tradition.

Disclaimer

Several of the treatments listed in this text are used today in modified forms. Holding myrrh under your tongue to stop a cough isn't so different from using aromatic throat lozenges. Mint still sweetens the breath in toothpastes and mouthwashes, and salicylic acid (originally extracted from willow bark) is the active ingredient in wart removal compounds. A practicing herbalist has informed me that peppercorns are useful against hoarseness, sage really does stop excessive salivation, and myrrh is still used in mouthwashes, toothpastes, and other products that soothe inflammation in the mouth.

Other recipes should definitely not be tried today. Throwing mercury on a fire to kill insects would probably work, but as AM434a also points out, the smoke is also highly toxic to humans. While it's true that warm compresses "draw out" boils, the use of freshly killed cats cannot be recommended, for reasons that I hope are obvious; hot moist towels are much more effective, much more sanitary, and much less cruel. And since one of the functions of gall or bile is to kill foodborne bacteria, animal gall should be effective against infections, but, well. . . yuck!

There is always uncertainty when one tries to interpret plant names in old manuscripts. Medieval authors were not modern botanists, and rarely described their plants with enough accuracy to make identification straightforward. They could be maddeningly vague; in one case the writer of AM 434a didn't even specify what plant should be used, only writing "herb that grows in wheat fields" (did he just mean "wheat", or would that be too easy?) When an herb could not be obtained locally, copyists were known to substitute a similar herb that could be had. Some names could refer to more than one plant; *centaurea* might have meant either of two unrelated plant genera, *Centaurea* (star thistles, cornflowers and knapweeds) or *Centaurium* (centaury). I've relied on Wilhelm Heizmann's *Wörterbuch der Pflanzennamen im Altwestnordischen* as my source for English and Latin equivalents of the plant names, but even his comprehensively researched work cannot always be clear as to what plant is intended. *Solsequium*, for example, could refer to dandelions (*Taraxacum* sp.), pot-marigolds (*Calendula officinalis*), or chicory (*Cichorium intybus*), while *súra* could mean common sorrel (*Rumex acetosa*), broad-leaved dock (*Rumex obtusifolius*), or, possibly, prickly lettuce (*Lactuca serriola*).

Diseases are not defined clearly in AM 434a. The text usually lists what modern doctors would call the patient's "chief complaint"— "headache", "darkness in the eyes", and so on. Except for the short sections of Galenic prognostics, the text almost never gives instructions on how to diagnose the illness any further; a medieval user of this text would not have known whether a headache resulted from muscle tension, a migraine, or a brain tumor, and probably could not have made much use of the information had he known. Scribal errors add an additional level of uncertainty; when the writer of AM 434a wrote *kolnnaa kuldaa*, "chilling cold", was it a mistake for *bolnæ koddæ*, "swollen scrotum"? Is the complaint *of sic* supposed to mean a prolapsed anus or a prolapsed uvula? Is ringing in the ears best treated with the gall of an ox or the gall of a pollock fish? In a few places, the text is so dense that I have had a hard time making any sense of it at all; I have done my best, but I have almost certainly introduced some errors of my own.

Finally, anyone tempted to try any of these remedies should bear in mind that the dosages are not always specified precisely in the manuscript. Like most drugs, many herbs are therapeutic at a low dose and toxic at a high dose. Others may have disagreeable side effects. Still others are easy to misidentify if collected in the wild; to give just one example, it is quite possible for an inexperienced field herbalist to mistake poisonous water hemlock (*Cicuta* spp.) for angelica, wild carrot, wild celery, or yarrow. Even a very safe herb can be dangerous if it causes an allergic reaction in a person who happens to be sensitive to it.

Hence this disclaimer is necessary: This text is provided solely for purposes of study, and is not intended to prevent, treat, or cure any disease. Neither the publisher nor the translator can recommend or prescribe any of these remedies. Persons with health concerns should seek the advice of a licensed health care professional.

Notes on the Texts

The text of AM 434a was published by Kristian Kålund in 1907, under the title *Den islandske lægebog*, "An Icelandic Medical Book." This is the text that I have used as the basis of my translation; I have not been able to consult the original, and as far as I know it has never been published in facsimile or in any other edition. For clarity, I have made a few minor alterations to the text layout from Kålund's published edition.

I have consulted three other published Old Norse-Icelandic medical texts with extensive parallels to AM 434a. The text of AM 655 XXX was published in 1860 in *Sýnisbók Íslenzkrar Tungu* [*Specimen-Book of the Icelandic Language*], edited by Konráð Gíslason. The text has since been digitized by the MENOTA project, and is available in facsimile, diplomatic, and normalized editions,[154] all of which I have consulted. The text of AM 194 was published by Kålund in 1908 as Volume 1 of his *Alfræði Íslenzk: Islandsk Encyklopædisk Litteratur [Icelandic Studies: Icelandic Encyclopedic Literature]*. Finally, the text of MS Royal Irish Academy 23 D 43 was published and translated in 1931 by Hennig Larsen, under the title *An Old Icelandic Medical Miscellany*. MS 23 D 43 is the only other Norse medical text to have been translated into English.

I have kept the spelling of all Latin and quasi-Latin words as they were published, and have relegated translations and annotations to the footnotes. In the text of AM 434a, I have translated all plant names into English equivalents, although I have left Latin names untranslated when they are followed by Norse equivalents. Appendix 1 gives my list of English plant names, the names in the original text, and the modern scientific names.

Several of the spells and charms at the beginning and end of AM 434a have parallels in later Icelandic grimoires and folk magical practices. Appendix 2 contains a few excerpts from volume 1 of Jón Árnason's great collection *Íslenzkar Þjóðsögur og Æfintýri* that are interesting to compare with AM 434a. I have translated his entire chapter on plant folklore ("Grasasögur") and selections from his chapter on magic charms ("Töfrabrögð").

I thank Dan Campbell and Thomas DeMayo for many helpful suggestions and much work proofreading the text, Dietrich Mateschitz for much inspiration, and Rebecca Radcliff for her store of herbal knowledge. Errors that remain are wholly my own.

. . . on five loaves of sacramental bread[155], and give him one each morning: on one loaf *bion*, on the second loaf *cerion*, on the third *agrionn*, on the fourth *sagirion*, on the fifth *enn-ducas*.[156]

Against tricks: *sans, gante, gantes, gantisim, gantissimus.* [157]

Against troll-riding: *res* ❖, *fres* †, *pres* †, *tres* †, *gres* †, "I expel from me ogres and ogresses, trolls and evil beings, I ask the sweetest lady Saint Mary that I may save both my own life and others', in the name of the Father and the Son." [158]

These tokens are against being ridden[159]: *G, Gi, Gina, Gisman, Gismand, Gismanda, Gismanndand.*

If men bear you ill-will, carry on you *ter, gramaton, alpha, edol.* [160]

For hardship caused by elves[161]: *In nomine patris Samuel et fili Misael et spiritus sancti Raguel.*[162]

Against the burning of a fire: *dixit mea Emmanuel Sabaoth eue omnes beatorem beata benedicti vos genntes peccatorum.*[163] Take your adze and strike a blow into the fire.

For a headache, carve *Misakx at rik sator arepo uere rotas*[164] on wood.

For swelling and inflammation in the skin, carve onto whatever you wish, *In nomine patris Annanias et fili Zacharias et spiritus sancti Sinnisael.*[165]

For weeping, carve on an oak stick *Funnde peccatoris verdum syna*[166] and let it lie on the altar during Mass.

For sleeplessness, carve this on wood and place it in the pillow under his head: *Res, refres, prefers, pregi, prodiui, esto labia uolunnt, post hoc dormivit.*[167]

For pain in the eyes, write on parchment *vau, nau, dele, neamon, aa-leph, gimel* and *anne*;[168] take three drops of milk from a woman who has a boy-child at the breast and add it to a raw egg, and let a man whom he has never seen before give it to him.

For headache, cut off the horn of a live cow and make a comb out of it, and then comb the hair of a man with a male cow's horn, but the hair of a woman with a female cow's horn. Crush it in wine or olive oil or water, and wash the head with it for nine days. Then it will get better.

Incense stops a hemorrhage from wherever it runs, both from the worst sores in the anus and from other places. And it doesn't let a bad wound grow, if it is tempered with milk and laid on. It removes fits from the head and drives away deceitful thoughts.

Parsnip is "mura" in Danish.[169] Its roots and seeds are good in medicine. If a man boils its root with a little honey and wine and drinks a lot of the parsnip, that is good against anguish and sickness, against wounds in the throat, late and early. Whoever eats it or carries it, poison cannot harm him, or a poisonous snake hurt him. If a man eats a lot of it, he gets an urge for women, and then he may have sex as much as he wants. If a man rubs a parsnip root over his teeth, then it heals a sick head and sore gums. If a man drinks much of it boiled, that is good against a scorpion's sting. If a man grinds a parsnip with honey, that is good against an overly swollen belly. There is no root that nourishes man as well as the parsnip.

You may send this blood-stanching anywhere you want, as soon as you know the name of the man or the appearance of the animal:

May your blood be stanched † *in nomine patris et filii et spiritus amen.*

> May blood be stanched for them who bleed,
> blood fell from God's cross,
> the Almighty endured fear,
> wounds they tortured sorely.
> Stand before the door where bleeds
> the blood of God's son, hear
> where the wound-sea is an ocean,
> for us you were tormented on a cross.[170]

My Lord, stanch this blood † *inn per libera me domini sanguinis lixta et sanguinis unnda sct sit stetid iordanis plum qdus in iordanis baptizatus consumatum est.*[171] Suffering is ended, may wounds close up, may your blood be stanched, N. Just as you, my Lord, stanched blood from your own wounds at the ninth hour on Good Friday, may your blood be stanched, N., whether bleeding from hostility or a nosebleed, and all blood be stanched, from wherever it runs, in the name of the Father and Son and Holy Spirit.

May the red blood be stanched
that I see running,
burning blood,
running blood.
Stop, blood,
the flood stopped
when the Lord died.
Hold back your death-blood.

With this blood-stopping, the Apostle Peter stanched the blood of Our Lord, and he bled neither outside nor inside. *In nomine.*[172]

So said the holy priest Bede: there are three days in twelve months, such that if a man is conceived then, the body of this man will not be destroyed before Judgment Day.[173] They are the night after St. Brigit's Day, and two nights after St. Paul's Day, and eight nights after St. Agatha's Day.[174] But there are three other days that must be very carefully observed; they are the first Monday after St. Mary's Day during the fast, and two days after the feast of St. Peter and Paul in Chains, and two nights after St. Sylvester's Day.[175] On all these days, no blood is let from people or animals, because then all the veins are full. But if blood is let from people or animals anyway, then he will die either at once or during that week; and the deaths of those men who are born at these times will be hard. So it is also, if men eat goose meat on these days; then they will be dead before 120 days have passed.[176]

The wise man Ypocratas wrote these matters for Aronkur,[177] concerning the ways in which he should protect and care for the body. At the beginning of the month of March, let blood from the right arm on the seventh day. At the beginning of the month of April, on the ninth day, for sight and health of the eyes. On the third day from the end of the month of May, let blood from your arm if you want to avoid fevers. If you pay attention to this, then you will not lose your sight, nor catch fevers, as long as you live.[178]

ᚨᛁᚨᛁᚠR : ᚨᛁᚨᛁᚠR : ᚼᛁRᚨᛁᛏᛁᚠR : ᚼᛁRᚨᛁᛏᛁᚠR : ᚦIRIᚠR : Carve these signs[179] on a stick or on a sheet of paper, and lay it under the table where you are gambling with dice, and read the *Pater noster* in honor of King Olaf. *Quia apud te propiciacio est et propter legeni.*[180]

3

If a man wants to know who has stolen from him, carve this sign on the bottom of a box, and grind up yarrow in the water as small as possible, and speak these words: "I desire, by the nature of the herb and the power of the sign, that I may see the shadow of the one who has stolen from me and others."

This is best against theft. *In nomine domine amen.*[181]

Take the herb called yarrow on the feast day of Bishop Jon,[182] and do not let the sun shine on it, and take it with all the roots, and read these words over it when the sun is in the center of the southeast, and get for yourself a cask with four hoops: *Qui te creauit qui perte latronem vel furenntem.*[183]

If you want your enemy to fear you, carry this sign in your left hand:

R R t. F. a. a. q F. o. q. q. b. g. X. v.[184]

You must write this on uterine vellum[185] and keep it on you at all times, and powerful men will always love you, so that they will never be able to deny you whatever you might ask for: y. l. x. e y. s. p. a a t d x m 1 l. G f p R.

If a man hates you, then take this writing and lay it under the man as he sleeps, and then you two will soon reach a settlement:

þ. q. c. g. q. Ɔ. g. g. g. g G. C. d. d. f. R. k h. l. m. s. m. b. t. [186]

If you lay these characters under a sleeping man, he will tell you what he knows that you ask him, about himself and others: n. M. m. n. o l. m. s. ⊞ . G. q. o y. z. a. x. a. ⊠ c. y. b. b. b. a. a a y. k. k. h. æ e æ.

If you want to make a man sleep, take milk and singed cat hair and rub them around the teeth of a sleeping man. If you want to wake him, take a chicken's egg and break it in his mouth, and he will awaken then and there.

If you want to avoid rulers' anger, go out before sunrise and speak with no man going home or at home, and take the herb called yarrow, and make your blood flow and sprinkle it all over the herb, and then draw a cross on your forehead with the herb, and thus go before your lord.

Against a sudden attack[187]: † *ophann* ⁘ *phaor* ⁘ *agla* ⁘ *alphaus*, touch it in anger, *in nomine patris et filii et spiritus sanctus amen.*[188]

Wash yourself in water three times and read the Lord's Prayer in between, and say this three times:

> I wash from me my enemies' hatred,
> the greed and wrath of powerful men,
> that they may happily come to meet me
> and look me in the eyes laughing.
> > I strike love with my hand,
> > I put an end to lawsuits for money,
> > I put an end to prosecution for money,
> > I put an end to the persecutions of the strongest men.
> May God look upon me, and good men,
> may they always see on me with joyful eyes
> the Helm of Awe that I bear between my brows,
> > when I strive against notable men.
> > May everyone in the world serve me in friendship.

Hold water in the hollows of your cupped hands.[189]

If you want to win at dice-playing, take your dice and bury them to the north of the churchyard for three nights, for three more nights to the south, and three to the east. Then place them on the altar under the cloth for three Masses. Then throw them up with your hands with these words: "I invoke you, Thor and Odin, by Christ the crucified, that you transfigure[190] these dice." And throw them up a second time and say: "I invoke you by Enoch and Elijah." And on the third time: "I invoke you, by Frigg and Freyja, by Thor and Odin, and by the holy virgin lady Saint Mary, that you, Fjolnir,[191] let fall that which I can throw."

Against a boil, wherever it is: *Ave per qvam benediction splendidit* †. *Ave per qvam malediction deficiet* †. *Ave sedens adam resurreccionem* †. *Ave lacrima, aue redemcio* †. *Aue altitudo in ascentibus umanis cogitacionibus* †. *Ave profunnditas in visibilis et angelorum oculis. Ave quæ es inperarmis saltum* †. *Ave qvem partus percrucem omnia. Ave stella de monstrans solem* †. *Ave vritus divine in carnacionis* † *Aue per quam creatura* †.[192]

There was a man named Ypocras; he was a wise man and the wisest of all healers.[193] He told his dearest friends, on the day of his own death, that they should lay his books, in which were the secrets of healing, under his head in the grave. A long time after his death, an emperor came by, and saw on the grave that the wisest healer that had ever lived lay there. He supposed that there was some money in the grave, and ordered his men to ransack it—but they found nothing there but these hidden medical books of his.

The first concerns headache. If a man has inflammation in his face and a pain in the head or a cough, and often presses his left hand before his breast and picks at his nostrils, he will die. If a sick man often sweats in his sickness, upwards around the head, that is a good sign; otherwise it is past hope. If you often see a sick man turn himself to the wall, that is not a good sign. If a sick man has closed nostrils and piercing eyes and hollow cheeks and lips turned inwards and cold ears, and often turns this way and that, turning his head towards his feet and his feet towards his head, know that the man will not survive, for men like this are sick to the point of death.[194]

In the month of January, you must not let blood. You should drink a cupful of wine or ale every day on an empty stomach. You shall take these drinks against swellings and inflammations, with herbs crushed up together in them; you should use ginger, and you should drink rhubarb.

In February it is good to let blood from the thumb, or to take a bath, and it is good to make use of purgative drinks and warm food. You should use agrimony with warm wine.

In March you should drink pennyroyal and boiled agrimony seeds and roots prepared together. Do not let blood. Do not take purgative drinks, because that strengthens fever.

In April, it is good to let blood and take drinks, eat meat, let a cupful of blood, make use of warmth. Rue cures a stomach-ache. And drink lovage.

In May, drink betony and burnet. You should scratch up the branches beforehand. You should make use of warmth and warm drinks, because heat warms a man's intestines. You should drink beverages. You must not eat the head and feet of four-footed beasts. Awaken early and eat early; eat agrimony and drink wormwood and fennel.

In June, every day you should drink a bladderful of water.[195] You should not drink ale.

In July, be on your guard against women. Do not let blood. Do not take emetics or purgatives. Use sage and rue.

In August, do not eat hot food, and drink neither ale nor mead, unless it is new. Do not let blood. Do not take purgative drinks. Do not eat mallows and cabbages, because the black sickness grows from that.

In September, eat whatever is edible, for all foodstuffs are of the right quality at that time, and you may enjoy them. And then let blood.

In October, take new wine and radishes, fasting. Drink cinnamon.

In November, avoid baths, and do not let blood. Do not wash your head with warm water. Drink hyssop and cinnamon for stomach aches.

In December, bleed your right arm, let a cupful of blood, because at this time all swellings are ready to come out of a man's body. Take meat and the seeds of mastic.[196]

At the beginning of every sickness, you should fast and eat vegetable foods.

For a nosebleed, bind the big toe on the right foot with a strong thread. Then it will cease.

For the same: take pig's dung and burn it in a clay pot, and blow it in a pipe into the nostrils.

For a headache, boil pennyroyal in oil and rub it on the sick man's forehead and temples and crown. Also, for the same thing: Place together a root of wormwood, male fern, and ivy, and the white of an egg; tie them in a linen cloth and place it on the head. Wash the head with salt and sour wine.

For a sickness on the crown of the head, take southernwood ground in honey and sour wine, and give it to the sick man; then it will get better.

An ointment for the eyes: wine with celandine and the down of a young dove[197] with sour wine. If the eyes run, take two spoonfuls of rue and one of honey and blend them together and rub on the eye. But smear a bleary eye with a fox's fat. The juice of wormwood and absinthe, blended with honey and milk, heals all eye sicknesses. Also for the eyes: the juice of centaury and a drop of honey, blended together. Also for the same: place the juice of male fern and fennel, equal amounts of each, in a glass vessel; dry it in the sun, and rub it on against the burning. If an eye is struck, take a leaf of agrimony with an egg white, grind it up and lay it on the outside.

In case the eye becomes clouded, take a live swallow and cut off its head with a glass knife so that its blood runs from the glass and onto the eye where it has clouded; then it will clear.

For the same: nine buck-goat's turds and nine laurel berries and five peppercorns and ink.[198] Blend them with honey and rub on the sick man's forehead.

Also, for the same: a fox's gall and honey, well blended together. Place it in the eye; then the darkness will be taken away, if it is on the eye. A buck-goat's gall works the same way.

Also for the eyes, take the dew from rue grown at home, and place it in a glass vessel and blend it with sour wine and put it into [the eye]. Also take hare's gall and put it into the eye. Then it will be cleared and the darkness will be lifted. Also, take the root of fennel, put it into the eye, then it will get better. Put it into the eye crushed and warm.

Also, for the same: the gall of a partridge and the juice of horehound. That drives out all darkness from the eyes. Also, take new cheese and lay it in boiling water and make a lump out of it and lay it warm against the eye; then it will get better.

Also, here is a remedy for sore ears: take sheep's gall and blend it with a woman's milk. That clears space in the ears.

This medicine is to help a deaf man: take green spruce wood and lay it in a fire, but collect the liquid that runs out and put it in a bladder with a spoonful of honey and two spoons of the juice of the herb called the houseleek. Blend these three ingredients together and strain through a cloth and keep in a glass vessel, and when you need it, place it in the ears. Then the headache will abate and hearing will improve.

For a toothache: take burned salt and rub it often around the gum; then it will get better.

For a pain in the breast: take rue and boil it in wine and drink it.

For a pain in the heart: take horehound and pennyroyal and boil in water and mix with salt and drink it, fasting.

For pain or darkness in the eyes: place balsam in the eye, or the gall of an eel;[199] that heals exceptionally well.

For a toothache, take cress seeds ground with the white of an egg, and rub it around the tooth; that will heal it. For the same, chew the root of juniper; that takes away the pain and makes the tooth firm, and it also heals it.

For a dry cough, late and early, drink sage and cover yourself up well.

For a pain in the heart, drink a vessel full of pennyroyal ground in old wine.

The herb called arum, which is spotted like a snake—that stops leprosy, but if it is eaten, then it kills worms, if they are growing in a man, and [cures] a boil.

Also, for a pain in the breast, drink the juice of fennel.

Also for the same, take two spoonfuls of horehound, southernwood, and hyssop with wine, and drink for three days.

For all kinds [of poison],[200] let a man eat radish every day, fasting.

For a wound: lay salt on it and give the man oil with wine to drink.

If an arrow is stuck in a man, it may come out this way: take thistle and grapes and the white of an egg and bind them on.

To brighten the voice, eat sage.

If a man cannot hold his urine, take the brain of a hare and crush it in wine and give it to him to drink.

If a serpent crawls in a sleeping man, then take a loaf of sourdough bread,[201] hot from the oven, and break it up and lay it on both sides and press it hard. Then it will come out.

For blindness in the eyes: take the gall of a partridge and blend a little of the man's excrement with it, and lay it on for nine days.

For a toothache, chew the root of yarrow while fasting.

For an epileptic seizure, take the red stone that is found in a swallow's belly, and let him always carry it. Then it will not hurt him.[202]

In case a man loses his speech, take dog-rose seeds and crush them and give them to him to drink.

For a toothache, take a grain of sea salt and lay it on the tooth socket. That kills the worm and eases the pain.

To brighten the eyes, take cow's milk or woman's milk and drop it often in the eye.

If a man drinks poison, then you must give him the herb called arum to drink. Then the man will never suffer from poisons or worms.

For a toothache, take hellebore root and grind it in sour wine and lay it warm against the gum.

For a pain in the nipple, take hellebore root with pig's urine, and lay it on; then it will get better.

If a man cannot sleep in his sickness, take sorrel seeds and bind them in a cloth and hang it in hot water. When it gives off a smell, give it to him to drink warm. That is good against the sickness called "delirium" [*frenetica*].

If he cannot urinate, let him drink sorrel seeds crushed in water.

If there is a blockage in a man's bladder, then take fox blood, and within three nights the blockage will be released, if you rub it all over the man.

For hair to grow, take goat hooves and sheep droppings and burn them, and grind them in sour wine, and rub this on the head.

For a nosebleed: the smoke of calf dung stops it.

For warts, rub hellebore seeds on them.

For burns, rub on oil, or fresh fat from a pig's paunch, and the white of an egg. Grind them together and lay it on.

For a sickness in the lungs: horehound and butter cleanses it, if a man eats them.

Drink betony early, with water; that brightens the eyes.

Against flies: take white hellebore and mix with cow's milk and set it out, and they will die or fly away.

For a spider bite, take ashes, grease and salt and blend them with old wine and rub on.

For hoarseness, take olive oil and add a raw egg and ground pepper, and eat this when you go to sleep.

For hair to grow, take juniper berries and olive oil and boil them in milk and rub on the head. For the same: bear's belly fat, with bacon and old wine. You shall blend them together and rub them on the head.

For a wart, take warm dove's blood and leave it on; then it will go away. Also, for a wart: take leaves of male fern and crush them and lay them on for three nights.

For childbirth, take mugwort[203] and lay it on the woman's vulva under her clothes; then she will deliver at once. But when the baby is born, then take the herbs away, so that the woman's intestines do not follow.

If a man drinks or eats a spider, take betony and weigh out a third of an ounce, moist, and give it to him to drink. Then he will not get sick.

10

This has often been tested.

For the bite of a mad dog or wild animal, take the bird called a magpie and boil it in water and give it to him to eat, with good wine. Then he will not get sick.

For a hemorrhage, take mules' hair and burn it and give it to him to drink often; then the bleeding will decrease.

If a man's arm swells up with blood, let him take white flour and honey and milk and make a plaster of them, and lay it on for three nights. And if it does not abate, then hang the arm up and warm the hand, and warm up olive oil and smear it gently and often, all the way down to the armpit and up to the wrist, and then it will get better.

Again, for the same: Boil beans in wine and water and add tallow, and place them in a linen cloth and lay it on.

If hair or beard is lacking, then take the hairs that grow within the thighs of a donkey, which are found in winter and not in summer. Burn them, and take the powder and blend it with old oil from an olive tree, and smear that where you want. It works so well that even if you rub this on a woman's cheek, hair will grow.

If you want to test the strength of a stone, then take a vessel full of water and tie it on the outside, and it will draw out every mouthful.

Many of those matters found in cures turn out to be one sort or another which are not as well tested as this—and they will also be effective against coughing illnesses—though they have read much about these matters, yet they do not believe that they are more trustworthy than this one, because Alexander the great king sent that to his mother, and it's not beyond belief that he saw and tested it himself.[204]

For leprosy, take the stone that is in the head or heart of a swallow, and grind it and blend it with wine and give it to children to drink before the sickness gives them sores.[205] Then it will do no harm.

For a headache, cut a horn from the head of a live cow and make a comb of it, and comb the head of a male person with a [comb from a] male cow, but [comb] a woman with the horn of a female.

For poison or a poisonous drink, take sorrel seeds and crush them in water and drink it on an empty stomach, or eat while fasting through the night. Then it will not do harm, even if you drink poison a day later.

For a burn, take a white lily root and clean it well, and boil it a lot in water. Then pour off the water and mix it with the white of an egg and place it in a linen cloth, and lay it on frequently.

Also for a burn, take bark from an elm and burn it all together cleanly, and lay the ashes on the burn; then it will heal and leave no scar.

For a toothache, take the root of male fern and boil it in wine and keep it in the mouth. Then it will ease the pain.

Also for a toothache, take sour wine and sulfur and boil them in olive oil and rub this around the tooth. Then it will get better.

For a snakebite, take the warm flesh of a freshly killed chicken and bind it on. Then the venom will be drawn out.

Also, for the same thing: take the herb that is called purslane, and collect earth and bind it on. That repels snakes and venom from a man. This herb has the power that if you lay it all around any snake, then it won't dare to move from its place.

In case a baby is dead inside a woman and cannot be delivered, take summer savory with its seeds and grind it in wine. That forces out the dead baby.

Also, for the birth of a baby, take a cabbage leaf and bind it on the woman's right foot. Then she will deliver.

For all kinds of venom or poison, eat the herb called radish every day, fasting.

For darkness in the eyes and spots before the eyes, take the juice of male fern and pepper and rub them on often, for three days.

Also for the eyes: take the stone called *calamitatis*.[206] Place it in fire and burn it for five days and five nights, and when it is glowing, place it in sour wine until it cools, and then place it in a fire and roast it until the stone is powdered, and press it through a cloth. And take cumin and peas and laurel berries and cloves and juniper and grind them all and strain through a cloth. And lay the powder in the eyes. That will undoubtedly heal.

Boil the herb called "ambrosia"[207] in apple juice and drink it. That stops unmanliness[208] and all lusts.

Take a woman's milk and pour it into urine. If it floats, then he will live, but if it does not float, then he will die.[209]

Against insanity, take the herb called peony and bind it on the neck of the sick one.[210]

The herb that is colored like a snake[211]—take the roots and crush them in warm wine and drink them. That drives all kinds of poison out of a person.

Dock ground with honey is good for the eyes.

The forest herb called centaury, blended with honey, takes [darkness] from the eyes, if it has drawn over them. And a powder of this herb, drunk with wine, heals a snakebite.

The juice of the herb called yarrow, drunk with wine, clears a man's urine, even if it was formerly undone or unclear.

For a wound, take an eggshell and burn it, and a spoonful of honey and an equal amount of butter, and rub it on and crush up everything together. This remedy is good for wounds.

If a wound has grown together and has become diseased all around, then take cheese; then it will be opened.

But if a wound is old, take goat turds and boil them in old wine or in goat's milk, as much as porridge or cabbage. Lay that on the wound. That will heal, even though it may seem hopeless to the healer.

Also, yarrow, crushed and laid on a wound, heals every wound remarkably well.

Also for a wound: take iron rust and male fern and crush it all together and [lay it] on. That heals well.

Crush the herb called celandine very well, with fresh fat, and lay it on. That cleanses and heals well.

Also, for the same: take plantain and grind it with the white of an egg and lay it on a wound. Then it will be cleansed and not leave a scar.

Also, for a wound which opens up by itself, take the herb called horehound and grind it with old fat. That cleanses and heals very well.

Deer antler has power against many illnesses. For toothache, take burned deer antler and then grind it all together and rub it around the tooth. Then it will be made fixed, and will heal.

For gangrene, take the dust of burned deer antler, one ounce in weight, and a vessel full of wine and two of water. Blend them together and give this to the sick man to drink. This heals wonderfully well and quickly.

For all kinds of hemorrhages, take burned deer antler and crush it in wine and give it to drink; then it will decrease. [212]

If a deer's antler is burned where there are snakes, they will either die or flee.[213]

Also against snakes: take tallow and the marrow from a deer antler. That chases snakes away and heals snakebite.

For pain in the eyes or pain in the feet: take a hare's lung and bind it on the eye or feet if there is a pain in them. It will cease and soon heal.

13

To break up a stone in a man's bladder, take fresh hare's blood and the hare's freshly flayed skin and burn them. Take the ashes and place them in old wine and give three spoonfuls to the fasting man each day. Then the stone in the man will break up, and it will heal him. If you want to test it, take a stone and lay it in this drink, and it will melt within three days.

To grow hair, take a hare's belly, boiled in oil. That makes the hair shiny and makes it grow.

For the ears, take a fox's gall or fat and pour it in the ear. That takes away pain.

But fox's gall with honey takes darkness from a man's eyes.

Pour goat's gall ground up with honey into the ears. That heals them well and takes away toothache.

Drink a boiled buck goat's turd with wine; that relieves all sicknesses.

Burned ox horn drives away all snakes.

For the eyes, take wine and oil, salt and soap, and blend them together in a basin and let them stay there for three nights, and then filter it through a linen cloth and collect it and place it in the ears when necessary.

Also for the eyes: take the dung of a goshawk and grind it with wine and honey in a basin; it is good for the eyes.

For a pain in the eyes, take garlic and radish and salt and pitch or tar, and boil everything together. Make a plaster of this and lay it on; then it will get better.

For unmanliness,[214] take the worm that shines in the night, crush it in wine and drink it; then it will go away.

In case the uvula falls, take nine beans and warm them, and pick up each one with a stylus, as warm as you can stand, and hold them on the uvula; then it will get better.

For the worm that crawls around the heart, take the scape of an onion and wormwood and eat them often, fasting.

For darkness in the eyes, take ink and honey and eel's gall and blend them together, and leave them in a vessel until you need to place it in the eye.

For a headache, take male fern and boil it, crushed, in wine or ale or water, and wash your head with it for nine days. Then it will get better.

For a spot in the eye, take honey and strain it through a linen cloth. Drop three drops into the eye every day. Then the spot will go away and the eye will heal.

In case the eyes grow heavy with blood, take wormwood and woman's milk and crush them together and wring them through a linen cloth. Place this in the eye often.

In case a woman cannot give birth to her child, take woman's milk and olive oil and give them to her to drink. Then she will quickly be delivered.

Also, for the same thing: take the herb called mugwort and bind it on the vulva.[215] But when the child is born, take the herb away quickly, so that the intestines do not follow it. This has often been tested.

If you want hair to grow in a place where it has disappeared, take a woman's hair and burn it, and blend it with honey and make a plaster, and lay it on where the hair has gone. Then hair will grow and never be lost.

For a nosebleed, take the shells of eggs that young birds have hatched out of, and powder them and blow them into the nostrils. Then it will be stanched.

Also, to stop bleeding, take the herb called celery, and crush it and squeeze out the juice and give it to drink.

For a quarrelsome and ill-tempered man, take celery and give it to him to drink. Then his anger will soften and happiness will come about, and his temper will improve.

If a man cannot hold his urine, take dock seeds and grind them in water and give it to him to drink, and give him a roasted goose tongue to eat.

For hoarseness, take horehound, which is an herb, and squeeze out the juice, and take an equal amount of sour wine and a like amount of honey, and blend them together and give it to him to drink often. Then his voice will get better. For the same: let the man hold ground pepper for a long time in his mouth, and then swallow it down with the saliva, and let him take olive oil or another fat. That is good for the voice.

For a man who has lost his wits: take "follow-the-sun"[216] and southernwood and sage. Grind these three herbs in wine and give it to him to drink for three days or five.

15

For a wound, take the skin from bacon, and honey, and the juice of the herb called celery, and white flour, equal amounts of each, and make a paste of them and lay it on the wound. That heals it quite well.

For a boil, take sulfur and ink and doves' dung, equal amounts of all, and grind them with honey and sour wine and bind it on.[217]

For a toothache, take garlic and crush it without salt and lay it on the gum or in the tooth socket overnight; then it will get better.

For swelling of the belly: take the herb called pennyroyal and boil it in wine or in ale and give it to him to drink, warm in the evening and cold in the morning. Then it will go down.

For a tooth that always aches, take shavings of a stag's horn and boil it three times in meat broth[218] and let the boiled horn be wrung through a cloth. Take a mouthful of this often, and keep it in the mouth for a long time before you spit it out. That makes a tooth painless.[219]

For sleeplessness, take the herb called opium and crush it in sour wine and smear it over the man's entire body, and give him sorrel[220] to eat. That makes him sleep quite well.

For snakebite, take the juice of plantain and olive oil and salt and give it to him to drink. That forces out the poison.

For a broken bone, take a chicken and grind it all up, with the feathers, and bind it on. That heals the most rapidly.

For an excessively fat belly: Take rye bread, not blended with other grains, and break it up in wine or another beverage, and let it stand for seven more nights; then drink of it every morning and every evening for twelve months. Then you will grow thin.

If a boil appears on a man's arm, then take a cat and kill it and stick your arm in it, if it is warm, and then bind it on until the next day, and do so for three days if necessary, and every day take a live cat. But if it is in another place in a man's flesh, then bind on warm freshly-killed cat's flesh until it is cold. That draws a boil out of man's flesh anywhere.

For pain in the eyes and dimming of the sight, take a live eel and cut it and take both blood and gall out of it, and blend both together and place it in the eyes. That brightens a man's sight.

For a hemorrhage, take the herb that grows in wheat fields, with its own leaves and red seeds, and crush them in wine or ale, and meanwhile sing *Pater Noster* and give it to him to drink.

For the hemorrhage if a wound bleeds, take a "night-leek" and grind it well and lay it on the wound and bind it on.

For a swelling in the breast, take plantain and bind it on.

If you want to restrain yourself from carnal lust, take the herb called rue and eat it frequently. Then it will be eased.

For snakebite, take rue and bind it on.

For a headache, take rue and grind it in olive oil and rub it on the forehead. That takes away the pain and improves the eyes. This has often been tested.[221]

For a pain in the loins, take the herb called centaury and grind it in water and drink it cold, often.

In case a man is thirsty, take centaury and grind it in water and drink it boiled.

For a wound, take the powdered herb called centaury and sprinkle it on the wound. That heals and cleanses it.

For an ache in the eyes, take the root of the herb called vervain and leaves of the herb called fennel and grind them both together and place them in the eyes.

For darkening of the sight: Take the herb called creeping thyme and grind it well and drink it while fasting. That improves and brightens the eyes.

For excessive flow of tears from the eyes, take sorrel and blend it with old wine and keep it in a glass vessel and make use of it often.

For a bad smell in the nostrils, take the juice of mint and pour it in. That takes the stench away.

For darkening of the sight, take wormwood and grind it well, and take an egg and hard-boil it. Then cut it in two and take out the yolk and lay the crushed wormwood in its place, and when you go to sleep, then lay as much as you may have on the outside of the eyelids. That clears and brightens the eyes.

The herb called woad—dry it and powder it, blend it with wine and give it to a man to drink. That breaks up stones in a man's bladder.

Green sweet gale, ground well and blended with sour wine, is good to wash the head with.

Lay the herb called acacia against the rectum if it prolapses: then it will turn itself back; and also a wound if it becomes inflamed.

The herb called *rubea*, which is madder, expels a child from a pregnant woman, even if the child is dead.

Earth, on which a seal is laid with a man's likeness on it, is good against snakebite and other flying snakes.[222] And if a poisonous drink is given to a man, then he should drink this earth: it drives out the poison, and it does not harm the man.[223]

The stone called *choralius* is good for the eyes and darkening of the eyes.[224]

Balsam improves darkness of the eyes and cleanses them.

Incense stops a hemorrhage wherever it runs, and it alleviates foulness in the rectum, or else doesn't let it grow in another place. If it is tempered with milk and laid on, then it is a healing treatment.

Diaskorides[225] says about the herb called peony: "I saw a boy, seven years old, who had that herb hung around his neck. It so happened one day that the herb fell from him. Just at that moment the boy fell down and had a seizure. But when it was hung back on him a second time, the boy wasn't harmed while he had it on himself. But then it fell from him a second time, and immediately he fell in the same illness that he had had before. Then the herb was tied onto him again and he got better immediately. And it happened the same way the third time: he grew worse when it was off, but got better when it was tied on." Galienus[226], the wisest man, gives the same testimony concerning this same herb.

The bark of goat-willow, crushed in sour wine, takes off warts. So said Galienus: sap wrung from willow bark, when the willow is in bloom, also brightens the eyes and does much good.

The juice of goat-willow twigs and flowers, if it is drunk, stops hemorrhage and hinders a woman from becoming pregnant.

Mint strengthens the stomach and makes the mouth smell good. But a plaster made of mint and salt is good against the bite of a dog.

The herb called white hellebore, blended with milk and tempered with honey—that kills a mouse, if it eats it. But a powder of this, blended with water and sprinkled around the house, kills flies.

The herb called cumin, drunk with wine, cleanses the bite of a flying insect. But if it is blown in a man's nostrils, it hinders a nosebleed.

The juice of the herb called celandine cleanses and sharpens the sight[227] and dries out the heavy humours in man.

The herb called rue kills lust in man, and cleanses the bite of a flying insect.

Mercury, when drunk, causes death, because in every member in which it flows, it erodes from the inside. But if it is laid in a fire, then it makes noxious smoke: serpents flee it, and insects die from the smoke.

Wormwood blended with ox's gall[228] and butter, and laid on a man's ears, strengthens them and drives out ringing in the ears. But if it is laid in a chest of clothes, then moths will not spoil them. And if ink is made from the water which wormwood is in, the writings will last: no mouse will dare to damage them.

For a cough, take the incense called myrrh and hold it under the roots of the tongue for a long time.

Also for the same, take the root of the herb called lovage and grind it in wine and drink it.

Also for the same, and in order to cleanse the lungs: Take eleven seeds from a willow catkin[229] and eleven peppercorns and eleven fennel seeds, grind them all into powder and blend with honey and eat a spoonful of this every day, fasting. This has often been tested.

Also for a cough, take the herb called burnet. Blend it with sour wine and give it to him to drink. Then it will help.

The herb called fennel—grind it in wine. That is good against a bladder stone.[230]

Also for the same, take rye bread and toast it in the fire, and eat it toasted in this way, with warm wine.

For pain in the side, take the berries of willows and ginger and use this in warm wine.

For a clear voice, take pepper and chew it and hold it in your mouth for a long time, and then swallow the saliva down and spit out[231] the splinters of pepper, and drink two raw eggs. When you go to sleep, the voice will clear.

For the same, take the herb called gentian, boil it and drink it boiled. That improves the voice. And if you want to chew it quickly, then is good.

Also for the same, take seeds of the herbs called celery, cumin, fennel, dill, and pennyroyal. Grind them down to powder and drink it in wine. And eat a live eel.

For pus[232] in the lungs: take the juice of groundsel, one eggshell full, and an equal amount of olive oil, and blend them together and drink it often, while fasting.

For a pain in the chest and belly: take that herb called summer savory, and drink its juice in warm wine, and smear it on often when you go to sleep. Then it will help.

19

The herb called horehound cleanses everything bad that enters the lungs, if it is drunk often. But for the same, and for chills and fever: take three drops of the milk of a woman who has a boy-child at the breast, and place them in a soft egg and let a man whom he has never seen before give it to him to eat. This has often been tested.

For chills and fever, take wormwood and agrimony and plantain, and meanwhile sing *Pater noster* and *Credo in deum*[233] when you take them up, and grind them with a little wine and honey and drink this while fasting for three days, before the shivers come over you again. This drink is for every day of the fever.

For the same, take the herb called pennyroyal, and boil it three times in meat broth[234] and drink it boiled. When the fever comes over you, this slakes the burning of the fever remarkably.

For fever and all sicknesses of men and cows, take the root of plantain and grind it in cold water and give it to a man or cow to drink; he will get better right away.

If a man becomes speechless, give him a drink of the herb called dittany, with wine. Then he will soon speak.

For the same: take the herb called pennyroyal and grind it in sour wine and make it even, and put it in a linen cloth and place it in front of his nostrils. Then he will speak just as quickly.

If an arrow is left in a man, or wood, grind the herb called dittany and lay it on. That draws it out remarkably well.

For pain in the heart, grind the herb called rue and bind it all around the head. For the same, eat the herb called pennyroyal often, fasting.

In case there is something noxious around the heart, the herb called burnet heals it.

For a poison drink: take deer marrow and place it in wine and drink it all together; then it will not be harmful.

Drink the herb called radish, fasting; it is good against a poison drink.

Also, against a poison drink, take the herb called betony and grind it in old wine and olive oil and drink it; that drives out the poison.

Also, for the same, take burnet and rue and grind them in wine; that is a drink. . .

Absinthium is wormwood. It strengthens the belly of every man who eats it or drinks it, but it is best for it to be boiled in rainwater and to stand for one day before it is drunk. It drives away roundworms[235], and allows a man to piss. [If] a man crushes it with vinegar and rubs it on himself, then fleas and flies will flee from him. It is good against jaundice and also for a man's liver, tempered with spikenard. If a man mixes vinegar with wormwood, it is good for the kidneys. If wormwood is blended with honey, it is good to rub on the eyes; then it clears them. Water from boiled wormwood is good for pain in the ears. Wormwood is good for fresh wounds,[236] if it is crushed and laid on. It also helps against itching, if a man washes himself in water in which it has been boiled. A man will also not vomit from seasickness, if he drinks it first. If a man crushes it and lays it on a swollen testicle, it helps that. If a man lays wormwood in bed next to him, then he will sleep well. It is also good to lay in books and clothing. If a man crushes it in honey, that helps with swelling of the tongue and the blue-black discoloration that comes onto the eyes. A mouse will not eat a book which is written using ink that is made from the water in which wormwood is boiled.

Aristologia, birthwort, releases the afterbirth from women. It helps with pain in the eyes and coughing if it is drunk with river water, and against every kind of pain if it is crushed and laid on. It also helps with epilepsy and with chills and fever, with sickness of the feet and stomach-aches, and it helps those with palsy.

Ambra, ambergris[237]: the best is that which is greasy and flecked. It strengthens the belly and wits and all of a man's limbs, most of all old men and those who have a cold nature, and most in the winter.

Alanum, alum, cleanses the eyes and makes the sight clear, and shrinks excessive flesh in a man's eyelids and in other parts, and doesn't allow bad sores to grow. Alum tempered with honey and vinegar fastens loose teeth and heals swollen gums. Alum heals blisters and scabs, if they are washed with water in which alum is dissolved. Alum tempered with vinegar heals a sick belly and the sickness called scurf.

Acedula, sorrel, is good for loss of appetite and chases away the bad fire. When it is crushed, then it is also good to lay on swollen eyes and brows. Its juice, blended with roses, is good for coughs in the old. If a man drinks it with wine, it is also good against all kinds of catharsis. If a man eats it very often, it is also good against poison. If its juice is laid in the eyes, it makes them clear, and laid in the ears, it improves the hearing. If a man carries it on himself, then the serpent known as *scorpio* will not harm him.

Argentum vivum, quicksilver, kills lice and fleas, nits and flies. If a man makes an ointment out of it with olive oil and vinegar, it is good for itches and blisters. Any man who drinks quicksilver drinks his own death. If it is placed in fire, it is completely turned into smoke, and if this smoke touches a man's body, it damages it and makes it shiver and grow torpid until it is destroyed, and it causes depression and bad complexion, foul breath and bad health. Snakes flee this smoke, or else they die.

Basilica, gentian: all its power is in the roots. It is good for a sick stomach and a sick liver, and for sick kidneys, spleen, and heart, if he drinks it with wine, vinegar and honey or warm water. But those who have a strong body should drink it or eat it, fasting, and should cut it up small and drink it that way. If someone does this often, it is good for thigh pain, stomach cramps and coughs, pain in the torso and constipation in the belly, for dropsy and other spasms, for pain in the sides, and for those who spit up blood. It is dangerous when it is hollow, because serpents spit poison into it in the month of August.

Cupembe [cubeb] is just like peppercorns; it moderates everything between hot and cold.[238] It makes a man cheerful, with good breath from his mouth and belly. It helps well with skin eruptions and is good for headaches. It breaks up kidney stones.

Crocus is saffron. It removes sickness in the belly, makes the head heavy and lets a man sleep, and heals sore bowels, and it decreases looseness in the belly.

Enula, elecampane: If a man drinks it, it lets him piss well, and loosens the bowels and releases a dead infant from a woman. The crushed root is good to lay on sore thighs, and the boiled leaf is good to lay on for kidney pain. If a man eats the roots with honey, it is good for a cough.

Ferrum, iron, glowing hot and quenched in water, is good for skin eruptions and swelling of the spleen. Rust from iron strengthens the sinews and heals the flesh that grows from below in a man's backside[239]; it also restrains a woman's hemorrhage and hinders conception. Boiled in vinegar and dripped into the ears, it makes them better. If a man drinks that, he becomes sluggish. If a man drinks iron rust and does not take a small amount of lodestone tempered with wine, then he will die. Tempered with vinegar, it is good to lay on a dangerous inflammation. It is smeared on a scurf-covered head where the hair grows.

Galiga [galangal] is hot; it is good for a cold stomach and digests food, and gives off a pleasant smell and creates lust for women. It also helps against cold.[240]

Licorcia is licorice. It is fittingly hot and moist. It is good for coughs and helps a man's chest and throat and also the lungs, and it diminishes thirst. It also helps the chest and all the spaces for respiration.

Mirtius, sweet gale—its aroma stops fits in the head. Crushed gale dries moisture in the ears and kills large worms. Dwarf gale is good against hemorrhages and other flows. Green gale, crushed in vinegar, stanches blood if it is laid on the head.

Piper, pepper, is hot and dry. If a person's dung is burned and added to ground pepper, it is good in case the person's mouth is inflamed. Pepper is good for toothache if it is crushed and then laid against the sore tooth. Pepper helps a cough, a sick liver, and a cold belly, and decreases pain in the sinews. It cleanses the chest and is good for stomach cramps. Pepper loosens coldness and moisture that exist in a person's belly. Pepper blended with eggs clears darkness of the eyes, if they are smeared on. If pepper is crushed with olive oil, it is good to smear the body with this, against the shivers.

Pix liqvida, pine-tar, is hot and dry in the third degree.[241] If a person takes a full spoon of it and another of honey, that is good for a long illness[242] in the chest, and fever, and labored breathing. If a person eats it with olive oil and almond kernels, that dries up fluid in the ears, if it is in them. If a person mixes salt into tar, it is good to lay on the place where inflammation has entered. If it is blended with wax in equal amounts, it heals impetigo sores and softens the hardness in them. If it is blended with sulfur, it helps against the illness called scurf. Pitch is quite helpful for these same conditions, and is good to add to plasters and ointments for applying.

Sinapis is mustard, hot in the fourth degree, but its seed is even hotter. Mustard gives a person sharp wits and loosens the chest and breaks up kidney stones. Mustard crushed with hot water and placed in the mouth, so that it rests for a while in the back of the throat until the person begins to sneeze—that clears the head. If a person eats mustard, it strengthens his belly. Crushed mustard with vinegar cleanses the bite of a viper. If a man crushes mustard seed and the soft part of wheat bread, so that there are two parts of mustard to one part bread, and adds that to dried figs and honey, the hotter the better, and the man adds more figs than bread, it is good for the head and eyes, lungs and belly and cough, pain in the thighs and in the bladder. If oil is made from mustard seeds, it is good for pain in the loins and sinews. The smoke from mustard is good for seizures. Mustard seed crushed with figs is good to lay on the newly shaven head of one who is insane, and also if a man smears his feet with it. If a man crushes mustard seed with some butter or fat, this is good for baldness. If a man eats mustard before chills and fever take him, it helps.

Sal is salt. There are four kinds, all hot and dry, some more than others. Salt deepens the color of gold and makes silver white, if it is washed with it. If a man lays salt in a bad and large wound, then it will not become larger. If a man places salt in oil, it is good for smearing the limbs where there are pains from exertion. If a man crushes salt with hyssop and vinegar and lays it on the sore place that is called scurf, then it will not spread any further. Salt is good for a prolapsed rectum.[243]

Here it begins: A steam bath is good for those who have dry and twisted limbs, and it is necessary for them to become moist. For that reason, a man must take great care to have it not too hot, nor to make his nature and body sweat much, and not to dry out too much. But he may be there until he has beaten[244] and sweated his flesh and body somewhat, and then he must no longer have hot water on himself.

A steam bath does these good things: It moistens the body and opens the sweat pores and washes away filth and decreases the foulness that the body has. It loosens the humours and helps one sleep well. It makes blood thin which was thick before.

A steam bath does these harms: It diminishes a man's strength and sometimes makes the heart so hot that the man falls unconscious from it.

A steam bath makes a man nauseated and gives some men cause to die suddenly, and for that reason, men who have wounds, fever, swellings, or fractures must avoid steam baths. A man should not go into the steam bath after a meal, unless he wants to become fat. A man should also not eat at the time when he comes out of the steam bath, but rather wait for a good while after.[245]

So said Master Ysodorus: the shape of a human body is formed in its mother's womb.[246] In the first month, blood and flesh are joined together.

In the second month, the joints and limbs for all the body come into existence. In the third month, the bones and sinews are strengthened. In the next month, nails and hair grow. In the next month, the baby comes to life upon the arrival of the soul.[247] In the next month, the baby stirs, from which the woman then feels heavy in her body and ailing. In the next month, the baby begins to have the likeness of its mother and father. In the next month, it only grows and develops. In the next month, the fetus awaits the divine design. In the next month, it enters the world as God has ordained.[248]

> In every man's mouth are teeth and tongue,
> marrow in bones,   blood in vessels,
> strength in sinews,   sight in eyes,
> hearing in ears,   smell in the nostrils,
>> snorting in the nose and in hungers,
>> snot and coughing in the lungs,
>> sense and memory and understanding,
>> wit and thought in the heart,
>> redness in the lungs' passages,
>> the sound of the voice in the windpipe.
> A man makes speech   with mouth and tongue,
>> with teeth, lips, and palate.
> Man has hate in the liver, but jealousy in the bile,
>> lust in a man's loins,
>> but in a woman's belly below the navel.[249]

No woman who does not menstruate may conceive a child.

Various things cause fields to become unfruitful. Sometimes the seed or the soil is the cause, sometimes the weather or lack of care, so that it becomes both too hot and too cold, and thus too wet. Infertile people are also like this, women just like men: some have enough of these things, but some have little. Some have the seed of lust for procreation in themselves, yet nonetheless live in moderation. Some have desire in the body and never release it, and yet have frequent desire to. Contrary to this, says Ysodorus, [are] men of a cold nature.[250] Some become too hot in their character and release it before coming to the intended place on the earth. Some are excessively fertile and determinedly sow in the same earth, and infertility does not grow up.

25

Sator arepo tenet opera rotas.[251] *Machumetus in labora lago per sanctam virginitatem Marie que portauit Iesum Christum de utero suo per verbum Gabrielis archanngeli.*[252] You shall read these words three times over the woman's loins and make three signs of the cross every time: *in nomine patris et filii et sancti spiritus amen.*[253]

The cross of our lord Jesus † Christ, which I ask this of. The cross of Jesus † Christ goes over all swords. The cross of Jesus † Christ over a still lake †. The cross of Jesus Christ is a wondrous sign †. May the cross of Jesus Christ preserve my life †. Cross of Jesus Christ, guard my ways in all virtue †. In the name of the holy cross I walk in all ways †. May the cross of Jesus Christ be sanctified over me †. Cross of Jesus Christ, take all evil from me †. Cross of Jesus Christ, take all suffering from me †. The cross of Jesus Christ makes me whole,[254] and may it be with me and before me and after me this day, and wherever the old enemy sees me, may he flee from me in the name of our lord Jesus Christ †. Jesus of Nazareth, King of Judea, bless me. Jesus, he went walking among them. Lord Jesus, crucified son of the living god, bless me and lead me to eternal life, God shelters me, may Christ protect me, wherever I am, may he protect me from all evil in the name of the Father and Son and Holy Spirit.[255]

First night of the moon: It is always good, and every man who gets sick will lie for a long time, and dreams shall turn out for joy.[256] Every child born will have a long life.

Second night of the moon: It is good to buy and sell everywhere and travel on a ship, and theft shall quickly be found out. Sick men shall quickly become healthy. A dream shall come to nothing.

Third night of the moon: No work shall get started, except misery will spoil it. Thefts will be quickly revealed, [and] those who have stolen. Dreams are of no use, and whoever gets sick then will not survive. Every child who is born will not thrive.

Fourth night of the moon: It is good to begin all kinds of labors and crafts. Sick men will be well soon, or never. Dreams are distinct, though they be slow to come true. The children of powerful men, if they are born, shall rule lands.

Fifth night of the moon: It is not good to begin, and he who become sick shall soon die. Dreams mean something, although they will come true slowly. A child will be blessed and long-lived, if he is born.

Sixth night of the moon: It is good for healing. A sick man shall lie for a long time; dreams shall come true. A child shall live long and be blessed.

Seventh night of the moon: It is good for healing. A sick man shall get up. Dreams will come true, although slowly. A child shall be good and long-lived.

Eighth night of the moon: It is good to move one's cow. A sick man will lie for a long time and not get up. Dreams will soon be proved. A child shall always grow and soon fall down.

Ninth night of the moon: It is good to begin all sorts of things. Dreams will come to nothing. A sick man will not live long. A child shall become a far-traveler.

Tenth night of the moon: It is the most good. Dreams shall come to pass on the third day. A child shall always grow.

11th night of the moon: It is always good. Dreams will turn out for joy within nine nights. A sick man shall lie for a long time and get up. The child will become gentle and good.

12th night of the moon: It is not good. Dreams will come true within nine nights. A sick man shall lie for a long time. The child that is born then will become a trader, and be short-lived.

13th night of the moon: It is always good to work then. Dreams will be revealed within twelve nights, for joy. A sick man shall lie for a little while. A child will become good in all respects.

14th night of the moon: It is not good to work then. Dreams are good. A child will live a short while.

15th night of the moon: Dreams will slowly come to pass and will be true. A sick man will lie for a long time and will live. A child will live long and wickedly.

16th night of the moon: Dreams will come to pass after the space of eighteen days. A sick man will scarcely live. A child shall be blessed.

17th night of the moon: Dreams shall be concluded within thirty nights and indicate danger itself; pray to God that they turn out for good. A sick man will lie for a long time and live. A child will die unbaptized.

18th night of the moon: You shall interpret your dreams as likely, and be on your guard within ten nights, and tell no more than two people, because dreams are good. A child shall live in great glory.

19th night of the moon: Tell your dreams to no other people; they will be resolved very slowly. A sick man will get well. The child that is born then will be good; he shall be blessed and a great warrior.

20th night of the moon: Whatever you see in dreams is good. It will soon be better for a sick man. A child that is begotten then will be the worst thief.

21st night of the moon: Every dream is true. A sick man will soon be well. The child that is born is wise in all respects.

22nd night of the moon: Tell your past dream, because it will be revealed in fourteen nights' time. A sick man will quickly be well. A child will be clear-voiced.[257]

23rd night of the moon: Your dreams will work out for your benefit. A sick man will die soon. A child will become a far-traveler.

24th night of the moon: Be wary of all your dreams; they will often be revealed within five nights. A sick man shall suffer great pain. A child shall be blessed.

25th night of the moon: Be wary of your enemies. Your dreams will turn out for comfort. Sick people will quickly get better. A child will become vigorous.

26th night of the moon: Be wary of your dreams, because they will turn out in various ways. A sick man will quickly become healthy. A child will not amount to much.

27th night of the moon: Dreams will turn out for joy. A man will be sick for a short time. A child will become unruly and disobedient.

28th night of the moon: All dreams turn out for joy. Sick people get better quickly. The child that is born then is gentle.

29th night of the moon: There will be dreams of some sort, coming true in nine nights. A sick man will never recover. A child will be excessively anxious.[258]

The manuscript's next two pages, and top of a third page, portray the following nine ring-shaped symbols. There is no explanation in the text as to what these are or how to use them, except for the uses written around the margins of each ring. Kålund points out a similarity with a set of magical signs called hjálparhringar Karlamagnúsar, *"Charlemagne's helping rings", described by Jón Árnason (see Appendix 2). There is also a general family resemblance to some magical "seals" that appear in Icelandic grimoires. I have redrawn these symbols for clarity. This drawing is not intended as a facsimile of the original manuscript:*

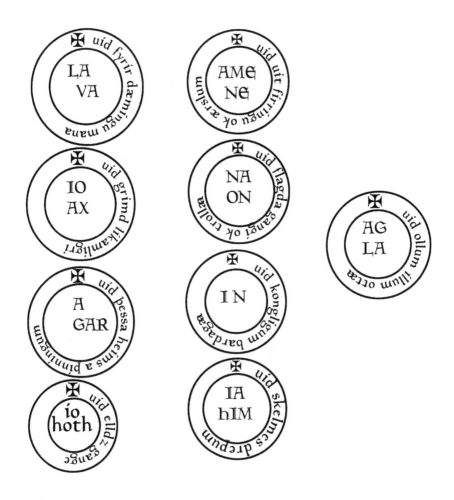

LA VA † against judgment of men[259]
IO AX † against physical cruelty
A GAR † against afflictions in this world
IO HOTH † against the course of a fire
AME NE † against madness and frenzy
NA ON † against the walking of ogres and trolls
IN † against kings' battles
IA HIM † against a demon's blows[260]
AG LA † against all evil terrors

Thus, frankincense, is hot and dry in the second degree. If a man crushes incense in pure or warm breast-milk, it clears the eyes and cleanses a fresh wound. If it is tempered with warm wine, it is good to place on the ears. For joint pain,[261] incense crushed with breast milk, and laid on the boils that appear below on the backside, helps that. If a man grinds up incense with the white of an egg, so that it becomes thick, and lays it on a fracture or on wounds which bleed a lot, and the man intends that the bone or wound join together, it heals it.

Place a sick man's spittle on a hot coal, and if it stinks, then the man will not survive. Or else let the sick man spit into water, and if it floats up, then he will die. But if the man lays his hands on his head and draws his feet up to his body, then he will live.

Thus spoke Galienus: These are signs of death in human bodies: if the forehead reddens, brows fall, the left eye contracts, opposite nostrils draw together or turn white, feet are cold, stomach sinks down to the spine.[262] Smear the feet of a sick man with meat and throw it to a dog, and if he eats it, then the man will recover; but if he abandons it, then peril is to be expected.

ᛏᛒᚼᚢᚠᚠᛂᛁᚠᚦᛦᚼᛁᚴᚠᛦᛦᛁᛏᚾᚥᛁᚵᛏᚦ [263]

APPENDIX 1: LIST OF PLANT NAMES

Names in the manuscript are italicized if they are clearly Latin, but left in plain text if they are Norse. English names in quotes are those that I have used in the manuscript in cases where the botanical identity of the plant is so unclear that no useful English equivalent exists for the manuscript name. All identifications are according to Heizmann's magisterial *Wörterbuch der Pflanzennamen im Altwestnordischen*.

English name	Botanical name	MS Name
acacia	*Acacia* sp., probably *A. nilotica*	*accacia*
agrimony	*Agrimonia eupatoria*	*aagrimonianum, aegrimonianum, agrimoniam, agrimonianum, agrimonie*
almond	*Prunus dulcis*	*alimandus*
"ambrosia"	either *Achillea millefolium* or *Artemisia* spp.	*ambrosia*
arum	*Arum maculatum* (wild arum) or *Dracunculus vulgaris* (dragon arum)	*dragontea, dragunncia*
balsam	*Commiphora opobalsamum*	*balsamum*
beans	*Vicia fava*	baunir
betony	*Stachys officinalis*	*betonica*
birthwort	*Aristolochia* sp., probably *A. clematitis*	*aristologia*, holurt

burnet	*Pimpinella saxifraga*; also applies to *Sanguisorba officinalis* and *S. minor*	*pipinella*
cabbage	*Brassica oleracea*	*caules*, kauli
celandine	*Chelidonium majus*	*calcedonia, celidonia*
celery	*Apium graveolens*	*apium*
centaury	*Centaurea centaurium* (knapweed) or *Centaurium erythraea* (common centaury)	*cenntaurea, centauree*
cinnamon	*Cinnamomum verum*	*cinnamomum*
cloves	*Syzygium aromaticum*	*gariophilum*
creeping thyme	*Thymus serpyllum*	*minna pulegium*
cress	*Nasturtium officinale* (watercress) or *Lepidium sativum* (garden cress)	*constensio*
cubeb	*Piper cubeba*	*cupembe*
cumin	*Cuminum cyminum*	*ciminum, cuminum,* komin
dill	*Anethum graveolens*	*anetum*
dittany	*Origanum dictamnus* (dittany of Crete) or *Dictamnus albus* (false dittany)	*diptamnium*
dock	*Rumex acetosa* or *R. oblongifolia;* possibly *Lactuca seriola* (prickly lettuce)	skogar-sura

dog-rose	*Rosa canina*	klungur
elecampane	*Inula helenium*	*enula,* holurt
elm	*Ulmus* sp., probably *Ulmus glabra* (wych elm)	alme
fennel	*Foeniculum vulgare*	*fenicule, feniculum, fetuli*
figs	*Ficus carica*	fikiur
"follow-the-sun"	various; possibly *Calendula officinalis* (pot marigold), *Cichorium intybus* (chicory), or *Taraxacum* sp. (dandelion)	*solsequium*
frankincense	*Boswellia carteri*	*thus*
galangal	*Alpinia officinarum*	*galica*
garlic	*Allium sativum*	kloflauk
gentian	*Gentiana* sp., probably *G. lutea* (great yellow gentian) or *G. purpurea* (purple gentian)	*basilica, genciana,* skarsæta
ginger	*Zingiber officinale*	*ingefer, inifri*
goat-willow	*Salix caprea*	selia
grape	*Vitis vinifera*	vinber
groundsel	*Senecio vulgaris,* but some texts confuse it with *Convolvulus scammonia* (scammony)	*senecciones*

hellebore	*Veratrum album* (white hellebore) or *Helleborus niger* (black hellebore)	*eleborum, ellebori, eboli, ellebore*
horehound	*Marrubium vulgare*	*marubbii, marrubio, marrubium, marubium*
houseleek	*Sempervivum tectorum*	*barbaiovis*
hyssop	*Hyssopus officinalis*	*ysopi, ysopo, ysopum*
incense	*Boswellia* sp. or *Commiphora* sp.	reykelsi
ivy	*Hedera helix*	*edera*
juniper	*Juniperus communis*	eine-berr, elne
laurel	*Laurus nobilis*	lava-ber
licorice	*Glycyrhiza glabra*	*licorcia*, sæti-vidur
lily	*Lilium candidum*	*lilio*
lovage	*Levisticum officinale*	*bilisticum, libisticum*
madder	*Rubia tinctorum*, but Harpestraeng often conflates this species with *Humulus lupulus* (hops)	*rubea*, rauda-gras
male fern	*Dryopteris filix-mas*	burkn, burknn, burknni
mallow	*Malva sylvestris*	*malvas*
mastic	*Pistacia lentiscus*	*mastior*

mint	*Mentha* sp., probably *M. spicata* (spearmint), *M. longifolia* (horsemint), or *M. aquatica* (water mint)	mintu, mynnta
mugwort	*Artemisia vulgaris*	buna
mustard	*Sinapis alba* (white mustard) or *Brassica nigra* (black mustard)	*sinapis,* mustardr
myrrh	*Commiphora* sp.	*mirra*
"night-leek"	probably *Allium* sp., although possibly *Platanthera bifolia* (lesser butterfly orchid)	nott-lauk
olive	*Olea europea*	oleo-tre
onion	*Allium cepa*	blot-lauk
opium	*Papaver somniferum*	*migo*
parsnip	*Pastinaca sativa*; could also be *Daucus carota* (carrot)	*astimaca,* mura
peas	*Pisum sativum*	erptr
pennyroyal	*Mentha pulegium*	*glietnarum, pulegium*
peony	*Paeonia officinalis*	*fioma, peonia*
pepper	*Piper nigrum* or *P. longum*	*piper,* pipar
plantain	*Plantago* sp., probably *P. lanceolat*a, *P. major*, or *P. media*	læknes-gras, læknis-gras
purslane	*Portulaca oleracea*	*portalego*

radish	*Raphanus sativus*, but possibly also *Armoracia rusticana* (horseradish)	*rafanum, raphanum*
rhubarb	*Rheum* sp., probably *R. rhaponticum* or *R. rhabarbarum*	*reponticum*
rose	*Rosa* sp., probably *Rosa gallica*	*rosaa*
rue	*Ruta graveolens*	*ruta, rutaa, rutan*
saffron	*Crocus sativus*	*crocus*, saffran
sage	*Salvia officinalis*	*salvia, silina, silura*
sorrel	*Rumex acetosa* or *R. acetosella*	*acedula*, sura
southernwood	*Artemisia abrotanum*	*abrotani, abrotanum, abrutanum*
spikenard	*Nardostachys jatamansi* (Indian spikenard) or *Valeriana celtica* (alpine valerian)	*narda*
spruce	*Picea abies*	greni
summer savory	*Satureja hortensis*	*saturea, saturna*
sweet gale	*Myrica gale*	*mirtius*, pors
thistle	various; in Iceland, generally *Cirsium arvense* (creeping thistle)	þistil
vervain	*Verbena officinalis*	*vervena*
willow	*Salix* spp.	vide, vidar

woad	*Isatis tinctoria*	*vitrum*
wormwood	*Artemisia absinthum*	*abscinnteo, abscintium, absinthium, sinthio,* malurt
yarrow	*Achillea millefolium*	*mellefolii, mellefolium, mellifolium, millefolium*

APPENDIX 2: ICELANDIC FOLKLORE

In his magisterial *Íslenzkar Þjóðsögur og Æfintýri*, Jón Arnason listed a number of Icelandic folk beliefs and practices that resemble some of those in AM 434a. I have translated his entire chapter on "Folklore of Plants" (*Grasasögur*; volume 1, pp. 641-647), followed by selections from his chapter on "Magical Charms" (*Töfrabrögð*, volume 1, pp. 428-484). All plants mentioned in "Folklore of Plants" have been identified as closely as possible using the on-line "Flora of Iceland" site.

Folklore of Plants

Just as oral stories circulate about unique animals, stories about plants also circulate; but much less is said about plant life than animal life. Stories about plants are much fewer, with less content, than stories about animals. I have only heard mentioned in oral tradition these plant species that will now be named.

Of species of trees, the most stories have come down about the **rowan tree**, for there has been a great deal of faith in it, both in old and recent times, and just as much all the way down to our days. It has had some sort of holiness about itself, and it's noteworthy that it should have saved Asa-Thor's life, when he waded the river Vimur to Geirrodargard. For this reason, the rowan has naturally been called "Thor's salvation" in honor of this event ever since, as the *Edda* says.[264]

Yet what is written about it in *Sturlunga saga* is even holier and more exalted: Geirmund Hel-Skin always saw a light over a rowan grove that had grown in a hollow, where Skards Church was later built at Skardsstrand.[265] Because he was a heathen man, this light was not to his liking. But as powerful and mighty a chieftain as Geirmund was, he didn't dare at all to uproot the grove of rowans. He only wished that he could eradicate it from his landholdings, but he wasn't able to do anything about it. And he beat his herdsman severely for having whipped his cattle with a rowan twig.[266]

In later times, the rowan has been considered one of the most trustworthy witnesses of innocence, since it has sprouted on the graves of people who have been accused and executed without proving their innocence in life. These stories are about that. It is said that in the old days, a brother and sister of good family lived in the Westman Islands. It so happened that the girl became pregnant on her father's farm. Because the brother and sister loved each other very much, loose tongues spread the rumor that the girl's brother must have impregnated her. This rumor also came before the lawman in the islands, and he went there to investigate the case. Although the brother denied committing this crime and testified strenuously that he was innocent, it was no use, nor that his sister exonerated him of all guilt and cohabitation with her, and named another man who at the time had left the islands. Since incest was generally prosecuted very severely at that time in the country, although the magistrates had nothing but false suspicions before them, each one passed the death sentence on the accused, one after another, and so it happened here. The brother and sister were condemned to death, and the sentence was carried out. But it is said that they both prayed to God, weeping at the place of execution, to prove their innocence after they were dead, even though the people had not wanted to believe it while they were alive. Also, they asked their parents to see to it that they could lie together in the country church graveyard. After that, they were executed, and after long grieving, and probably large contributions of money to the church and clergy, as was rather usual at the time, the parents were permitted graves in the churchyard for their children, but they could not both lie in the same grave. Instead, one was to be dug on the south side of the church, and the other to the north of it, and so it was done. When some time had passed, the people began to notice that a rowan sapling was growing out of each of the siblings' graves, and they rose upwards, always naturally, until their limbs touched over the crest of the church roof. It was assumed that, by allowing these rowan saplings to grow on their graves, God wanted to manifest the siblings' innocence before the living, since no one knew that any man's hand had planted them. And the fact that the saplings bent towards each other over the crest of the church's roof, and united their leaves and limbs, seemed to indicate the innocent and affectionate relationship between the siblings in life, and their desire that both might lie in one grave after death. These rowan trees grew and stood this way for a long time, until the Turkish Dog came to raid the Westman Islands early in the 17th century.[267] The Turks carried off both people and wealth, and committed many atrocities there, as is well known. One of these atrocities, as the story goes, was that the Turks chopped up both rowan

41

trees in the churchyard, and they threatened to return to the islands, with no less pillaging and raiding than when they came, as soon as these trees had regrown just as tall a second time. But the people have no report that the trees have ever sprouted after that, and that is considered God's greatest mercy, because if that had happened, the Turks would have fulfilled their words.[268]

Another story much like this one is current in Eyafjord, about a sister and brother who were condemned to death for incest and executed on Modrufellshraun.[269] They always maintained their innocence. As soon as they were brought to the place of execution, they prayed to God that he would at least prove their innocence after death. Then they were executed, and a rowan tree grew up out of their blood. It is said that many of these trees were formerly there, but now not a sapling is left in the district.

Many more stories are told of the rowan tree. It is called a holy tree, and the story is told that in the old days, when lights were brought to a rowan tree on Christmas Eve, they burned on all the branches, and they didn't go out no matter how much the wind blew. It seems that this must be some sort of image of a Christmas tree, such as is common practice in foreign countries to illuminate and decorate with fruits for the pleasure of young and old, especially on Christmas Eve, and which has come to be customary here and there in this country, in towns.

If a man intends to uproot a rowan sapling, and searches for it with that intent, he won't find it, even if he knows where it is supposed to be and finds it when he wants to at other times.

Rowan can hardly be used for any purpose. If it is used for firewood, it wakens resentment between those who sit around the fire, even if they had been the best of friends. If it is used to build a house, woman aren't able to deliver their babies in that house; neither can other creatures or livestock bear offspring or thrive. If rowan is used for building a ship, or for any of the ship's tackle, then the ship will be wrecked, unless juniper is used with it in the same ship.[270] If rowan is used for the oarlock pegs on one side of a ship, but not on both sides, then the ship will capsize. Concerning this last, it seems obvious why some common folk have said that "the rowan is cursed," since they haven't felt that it is safe to make use of it in any way, according to superstition. And it's very likely that that is the reason why it has been allowed to stand uncut ever since it has been growing in this land, and been left alone so much more than the birch woods, so that Eggert Olafsson said that it had grown six or eight ells high[271] along Hestfjord where it joins Isafjord,[272] when he traveled around this country in and after the middle of the last century.

Juniper and rowan. Although rowan wood cannot be used for shipbuilding, as was stated, there is no danger in using it for this purpose if juniper is used in the same ship. The reason is that juniper and rowan are the most powerful enemies. The juniper wants to pull the ship up into the air, but the rowan wants to drag it down into the sea—and this is good, because otherwise the ship would be driven over the seas, as it would be too free on the waves, if the juniper were in control by itself. But the rowan weighs the boat down, and so instead holds it reasonably firmly in the waves, whereas the juniper pulls on it from above. Thus one should have juniper in the gunwales, and rowan in the keel or the strakes alongside the keel.

Something else is said about the disagreement between these trees: if they are located on opposite sides of a large tree, they will pull the tree apart between them, splitting it lengthwise—that is how badly they get along. If juniper and rowan are in the same house, it will burn down. If a juniper and a rowan are on opposite sides of the same horse, the horse will get snagged. If juniper and "burning herb" [*brennugras* or *notrugras*; dwarf nettle, *Urtica urens*] are placed together in a chest at evening, each one will have moved to opposite ends in the morning.

About the **blood-oak** [*blóðeik*; any driftwood with a reddish color], it was previously noted that it may not be used in a ship, because that ship will be wrecked.

The **willow** has this nature: when it is kept in a living room or a farmhouse, a man is unable to die, nor can a woman bear a child. Nor can livestock bear their young, if a willow is kept in the barn. Neither can one carve or cut willow, because then the man will slice or cut himself and hurt himself, and all the wounds will heal slowly and poorly, if they heal at all, and it is said that it was a willow log from which Grettir suffered the wound that caused his death.[273] Neither does it seem safe to use willow for fuel, because as soon as it is lit, there will be such loud crackling in the fire that it seems unbelievable. For this reason it is customary everywhere that flotsam salvagers leave willows

43

lying uncollected on the beach, never rolling them away or paying them any heed, even if they should drift away later, because they feel that the willow is the worst tree in God's creation.

Thieves' root [*þjófarót*; mandrake, *Mandragora officinarum*]. Thieves' root is an herb with white flowers. It is said that it grows wherever a thief has been hanged, and it sprouts from the foamy fluid dripping out of the corpse. Others say that it grows up out of a thief's grave. The root of this herb is highly forked. When thieves' root is harvested, one has to dig out all the forks in it, without cutting any of them in any place—except for the middle fork or strength-root, which goes straight down into the earth; it has to be torn. But this nature goes with these forks: every living being that hears the screeching noise, as soon as it is torn, falls down dead. Thus those who dig up thieves' root tie felt around their ears. But so they may be more certain of hearing nothing at all, they take yet another precaution: they tie [string] around the root, and tie the ends to a dog that they have with them. As soon as they have made all their preparations, they run away from the diggings, and as soon as they feel that they have gone far enough away, they call the dog. The fork tears as soon as the dog obeys and intends to rush to the man; but the dog is killed on the spot where it hears the shriek of the torn roots. Then the root is taken and stored carefully.

This herb has this nature that it draws buried silver out of the earth to itself, just as the "sea-mouse" draws money out of the sea.[274] But first, one has to steal a coin from a destitute widow, and place it under the root between the Epistle and the Gospel readings on one of the three great holy days of the year. The root will draw no other coins than those of the same sort as the one that was stolen and placed under it in the first place; if that is, for example, an eight-shilling piece, it will draw nothing but eight-shilling pieces, and so on. I have not heard that there is any difficulty about keeping or losing this root; thus one may throw it away, wherever and whenever one wishes, with no consequence.[275]

Latch-herb [*lásagras*] or **four-leafed clover** [*fjögra laufa smári*].[276] This name goes with this herb because it opens every lock that it is brought to. There are two ways in which to accomplish this. One of them is for mares' placentas to be taken during the Moving Days, and buried in the earth next to a swamp, where it is rather moist, about a foot deep, and covered over with turf afterwards. If this is checked on St. John's Eve, the herbs will have grown. According to stories from Múlasýsla, where this herb is called "four-leafed clover", it should not have grown before the third year. Then one should take the clover and dry it in the wind, but beware of letting the sun shine on it, and wear it around one's neck on a silk thread. Then every lock will be opened for the one who has this herb.

The other course is somewhat more beset with difficulties. A man must make a complete doorway, with the door lock and latch, and set it in front of a wagtail nest, and lock it while the wagtail is not in the nest. As soon as she comes to the nest, she will want to get through to her eggs or young. Then she will seek out the latch-herb, and carry it to the doors, or stick it into the lock, and with that it will open up quickly. This is how men first discovered the nature of this herb. As soon as the wagtail is ready to carry the herb, one should take it and use it according to his needs and wants. But there is a difficulty that goes with it: the one who has the herb may never go bareheaded afterwards, because the wagtail will constantly be lurking nearby, to bring a poisonous snake to the head of this same person and kill him.

If a man falls asleep on "Mary's blouse" [Máríustakk; thin-stem lady's mantle, Alchemilla filicaulis], he will not feel fear in his sleep, nor have bad dreams.

Couples' herb [hjónagras] has two roots, one thick, the other sharp and slender. The thicker root inspires desire for women and bodily pleasure, takes away sorrow, increases joy and replenishes a man's soul-might. The sharper root should be given to a man for the sake of chastity. This herb is generally called "Brana's herb" [Brönugras], and there are still more names for it, for example, "love herb" [elskugras], "Frigg's herb" [Friggjargras], "lusty root" [graðrót] and "friend herb" [vinagras].[277] The name "Brana's herb" is evidently derived from the herbs that old Brana gave to Halfdan her foster-son, to gain the love of Marsibil, the daughter of Olaf king of England.[278] "Brana's herb" grows widely in Iceland, and the stalk is stiff and light green with leaves coming out from it in three directions, and the flower-head up above and purple-red, as Eggert Olafsson described it. Mohr recognized the superstition that people imagine, in Iceland as in other places, that this herb arouses lust and love between a man and a woman, and stills disagreement between them, if they sleep on it. But now it is most commonly said that the roots of this herb are powerful, and there are always two underneath one stalk, one hard and the other soft. Once they are cut off and both thrown into water, the hard one floats and the soft one sinks. As soon as a man wants to have this root to arouse love, the one who seeks love with it must dig deeply in a ring around the plant's roots, and pay careful attention that no branch of either root be cut off, once he takes it out of the earth; otherwise they lose their power. Once this is done, the man must lay one of the roots under the head of the one whom the man wants to gain the love of, but arrange it in such a way that the person knows nothing about it, so that she may sleep on the root, and the man himself must sleep on the other one. It is said that the man hardly ever fails to win the love that he is seeking, if it is correctly done.

Mead-herb [*mjaðurt*; meadowsweet, *Filipendula ulmaria*] is and has been used to find out who has been stealing. One must pick it oneself on St. John's Eve at midnight, put pure water in a basin with pure water, and lay the herb on the water. If it floats, then the thief is a woman, but should it sink, then it's a man. The shadow of the herb shows who the person is. One must read this incantation along with it: "Thief, I summon you back home with the booty that you stole from me, with as powerful a summons as God ordering the devils out of Paradise into Hell."

Freya's herb [*Freyugras*; meadow rue, *Thalictrum aquilegifolium*] is used to find out who is stealing from someone. First, one must let it lie in water for three nights, and then lay it under one's head and sleep on it, and then the person will see the one who has stolen.

Brook buttercup [*lækjasóley*; marsh marigold, *Caltha palustris*]. The nature of this herb is wondrous, for if it is picked when the sun is in the constellation of Leo (from July 13 to August 12) and washed in lamb's blood, and then laid there next to a wolf's tooth, and then wrapped in laurel leaves and carried by a person, no one is capable of speaking with that person except with peaceful words. If a person is robbed, and lays this next to his eye, the thief will be seen, along with everything he has done. If the marigold is laid in a house where there are women who are committing adultery, they won't be able to get away, until the marigold is taken away.

If **dark heather** [*sortulýng*; bearberry, *Arctostaphylos uva-ursi*] is kept in gray paper and carried on one's person, it protects the person from all ghosts, unless they are named. Dark-heather berries are called *mulníngar*. If people eat them, lice crawl off of them alive. For that reason, they are sometimes called "louse-*mulníngar*."

There are some more herbs that I know no stories about, and yet it seems likely that there are stories about them, or at least there have been. They are compounds with the name of the devil—for example, "drive-fiends-away" [*fjandafæla*; Norwegian cud-weed, *Omalotheca norvegica*]—and there's no need to do more than hear this name to show that great power goes with this herb, whereas it has previously been conjectured that it is a ward against evil. Others are "devil's finger", "devil's foot", "devil's herb", "devil's hair", "devil's cabbage", and "devil's rope".[279] Sometimes it's not possible to see whether medicinal power or magical power is the greater determinant of the names of herbs. So it is, for example, with "bloodroot" [*blóðrót*; tormentil, *Potentilla erecta*], which does in fact stop bleeding, yet which has been somewhat used in magical charms.

Magical Charms

[p. 448] Of these, I have seen that unaltered Latin letters have sometimes been used by themselves, sometimes together with rune letters in certain formulas, but probably most often in spells of warding. I want to first bring up a few examples which have been used in magic spells, before mentioning other letters. Here I shall first count the **sign against jaundice**, which is the letters in the remarkable and versatile magical verse which may be read in four directions and always ends up with the same first lines as the formula is named after, and which is called **Satorarepo**. Out of this verse this table is made:

47

S	a	t	o	r
a	r	e	p	o
t	e	n	e	t
o	p	e	r	a
r	o	t	a	s

All the letters in this verse should be carved on the nails of the sick one, so that his jaundice will improve. And this was used for many other purposes.

Another example is the formula to get one's request fulfilled. It is concealed this way: a man writes these words in Latin letters with dog's blood on his own wrist: "Max, píax, ríax", and then the one who was asked to offer help will not get out of it.

. . .

Now we turn to the runes, and analyze a few examples of those that have been used in magic spells, both the letters themselves, often used in complete arrangements, or complete words and formulas written in rune letters. But I believe it has been rare for one single rune-letter to be used in magic, unless it has been this one: ᚼ. This has sometimes been marked on horses' loins, either with tar or by clipping the loins. It defended the horse from suffering any damage, and it protected against lameness and injuries and horse sicknesses, against straying and theft by others. But whether this is a poorly made rune-letter *hagall* ["hail"], or rather, a magical sign, I shall leave unsaid.[280]

Next I mention the **woman's-spell**. In all likelihood this name results from that fact that men have made use of it when they want to attract a woman to fall in love with them. This formula was used for it:

I carve for you
Eight *áss*-runes,
Nine *nauðr*-runes, and so on.[281]

48

The second and third verses indicate that eight ᛁ runes at once were taken in the same place, and in the third verse, nine ᚼ were taken together.

There is the **sleep-thorn**, which is such an old spell that Sæmund's Edda[282] states that Odin had stuck Sigdrifa the valkyrie with this thorn, when she had felled King Hjalmgunnar, so that she could not manage to wake up. It seems that these runes were carved on a branch or sheet, and then stuck either into the hair or onto the breast of the one who fell asleep, and he could not break his nap by any means until the sleep-thorn was taken away, or else fell from his head or legs. The letter that has been used for this spell was ◊ [*sól*, "sun"], and it must have been very successful, but I do not know how often.

Next come **dream-staves**. Grunnavíkur-Jón does not mention either how many or which letters should be used for this purpose. These letters had to be written on a sheet of paper, and then laid under a man's pillow before he went to bed, so that what the man wanted to know would appear to him in his dreams. Those who have seen these letters in little books of magic say that the letters are 17 or 18 in all, and that they are not magic signs, "but most like some sort of scrambled alphabet, 'Peri's letters' or 'Adam's letters'."[283] One may see another example of rune groupings behind the printed "Busla's Prayer", at the far end of it; there appear five groupings of runes, in addition to which some manuscripts of "Busla's Prayer" have bind-runes at the conclusion, as will be shown later.[284]

As an example of how whole words and formulas have been written with rune-letters, Grunnavíkur-Jón brings up the formula against dysentery, and it reads like this: "Jesus Christus sat. ser. mundum liberavit"[285]; and the formula for winning at backgammon, which is like this: "Ólafr, Ólafr, Haraldr, Haraldr, Eirekr, Eirekr." The one who wanted to win had to write this formula on a sheet, and either keep the sheet on himself, or lay it under the backgammon board on his thighs while he was playing, and in addition read *Pater Noster* there for the holy King Olaf.

[p. 452] There were two other very common staves in the old days, which I have not heard the names of: both of them were used to see thieves, and both should be carved on the bottom of a basin. The first had to be carved with a basalt slab; one had to burn juniper to ashes and rub them into the carving, and pour water in the basin, "and you will see the thief." The other had to be carved on the polished bottom of a basin with magnetized iron; one had to pour holy water on top of it, and lay yarrow down on it.

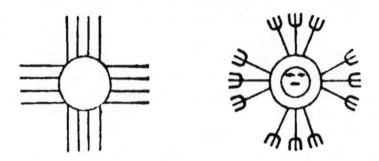

Next are two staves which should be carried on oneself against the malevolence of wicked men, and depictions of them follow as well. There is the **Helm of Awe** [*Ægishjálmur*]. It was cast in lead, and the lead image was fastened to one's forehead between the brows, as this spell shows:

> Helm of Awe, that I bear
> between my brows.

A man had to face his enemies with this sign, and then victory was certain for that man. It was an equally certain defense against the wrath of chieftains, and both this spell and the other spell whose verses went with it were proven. It goes like this:

> I wash from me
> my enemies' hatred,
> the greed and wrath
> of powerful men.

Grunnavíkur-Jón thinks that "Ægishjálmur" is a constructed name derived from the effect of the staves.

Deal-Closer [*Kaupaloki*] is the name of one stave; it gets good bargains for a man if it is drawn on rough paper and kept under the left arm so that no one may know. Grunnavíkur-Jón also names **Earth-Ox** and **Blood-Ox** [*Molduxi* and *Blóðuxi*]; they defend against theft, one by day and the other at night. I have seen no depiction of them. Three unnamed staves were used to raise the living dead, but I know neither their names nor their shapes.

Finally, I will give the names of three staves here: **Deceiver** [*Ginnir*], **Thor's Hammer** [*Þórshamar*], and **Ladle-Cross** [*Ausukross*], and illustrations of the first two are provided.

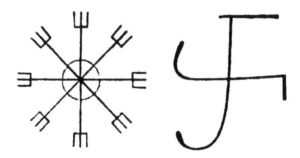

It is not known to me what the first two of the foregoing were used for, but the Ladle-Cross caused illnesses and many evils to those for whom it was carved. Its name is in all likelihood derived from its shape, because it is like the rune-letter *sól* [sun]with a cross-stroke over the ascender, like this: ⚔

I shall not even try to describe, even briefly, all the multitude of seals and sigils against various evils, but only set down here a description of

Charlemagne's Helping Rings, according to the books of magic in the state library. There it is said that God himself sent his angel to Pope Leo with them, and the Pope was to bring them to Charlemagne to defend against his enemies. These rings were arranged in three sets, and there were three rings in each. The first ring of the first set is protection against all the Devil's tricks, and enemies' attacks, and despair; the second, against sudden death and collapse, and all tremblings of the heart; the third, against enemies' anger, so that they shall quaver in their hearts when they see the one who has the rings; "they shall grow torpid and droop down." The first ring of the second set is against the bite of swords, the second ring against mockery and so that a man does not go astray, and the third against the wrath of chieftains and all persecutions by wicked men. The first ring of the third set gets one victory in court cases in a crowd, and the friendship of all men; the second is against all terrors; the third defends the body against lusts and luxury. These nine rings should be carried on one's breast, or on any other side where a man may expect to encounter his enemies.[286]

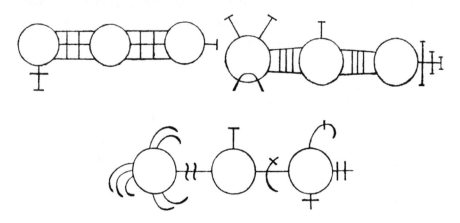

[p. 463] **To find out about theft.** Take meadowsweet itself on St. John's Eve around midnight. Fill a basin (i.e. a washbasin) with pure water. Lay the herb on the water. If it floats, then the thief is a woman; if it sinks, then it is a man. The shadow will show you who the person is. You must use this formula along with it: "Thief, I summon you back home with the booty that you stole from me, with as mighty a summons as God himself ordering the devils out of Paradise and into Hell."

Thief-summons. "I pronounce this for the thief who has stolen these things: may he go mad and swell up in great agony, and may he never have peace until he comes before me with the things that he has stolen from me. May Thor and Odin help." But if the thief has eaten [what he stole], then you must read this: "You shall spew up the things that you stole.

So shall your body
be fully bloated,
and everything be torn up
from the inside.
Now your guts
must howl,
all clawing each other
from the inside.
May I fall on you
with words so fitted,
that your breast and torso
may be burning,
as if hounds bit, tearing
around your heart.
May all your breast and mind become confused.
I forbid you to glance
at a holy book.
A branch shall come
out of your neck, worst boy,
and these true prophecies
shall still do you harm.
Vomit now
or else burst completely.
May Thor and Odin
be helpful in this,
so that the thief may have no excuse.

Carve these letters on oak wood and have them in your hand when the thief comes:

ᚠ ᚫ ᛔ ᛖ ᚳ ᛉ ᛜ ᛘ ᛏ ᛐ ᛞ ᛢ ᚱ ᚴ ᚹ ᚲ ᛚ ᚼ

BIBLIOGRAPHY:

Aalto, Marjatta, and Hanna Heinäjoki-Majander. "Archaeobotany and Palaeoenvironment of the Viking Age Town of Staraja Ladoga, Russia." Urve Miller, Björn Ambrosiani, Helen Clarke, Tony Hackens, Anne-Marie Hannson, and Birgitta Johansson (eds), *Environment and Vikings with Special Reference to Birka*. Birka Studies 4/PACT 52. Rixensart: Conseil de l'Europe, 1997. pp. 13-30.

Anthony, David W. *The Horse, The Wheel, and Language: How Bronze Age Riders from the Eurasian Steppes Shaped the Modern World*. Princeton: Princeton University Press, 2007.

Åsen, Per Arvid. "Plants of Possible Monastic Origin, Growing in the Past or Present, at Medieval Monastery Grounds in Norway." *Plants and Culture: seeds of cultural heritage of Europe*, Edipuglia, 2009, pp. 227–238.

Bang, Anton Christian. *Norske Hexeformularer og Magiske Opskrifter*. Kristiania: A. W. Brøgger, 1901-1902.

Barrett, J., Hall, A., Johnstone, C., Kenward, H., O'Connor, T. and Ashby, S. "Plant and Animal Remains from Viking Age Deposits at Kaupang, Norway." *Reports from the Centre for Human Palaeoecology, University of York*, 2004/10. 144 pp.

Behre, Karl-Ernst. "The History of Beer Additives in Europe—A Review." *Vegetation History and Archaeobotany*, vol. 8 (1999), pp. 35-48.

—. "Collected Seeds and Fruits from Herbs as Prehistoric Food."

Vegetation History and Archaeobotany, vol. 17 (2008), pp. 65-73.

Brombacher, C. "Archaeobotanical Investigations of Late Neolithic Lakeshore Settlements (Lake Biel, Switzerland)." *Vegetation History and Archaeobotany*, vol. 6 (1997), pp. 167-186.

Buhner, Stephen Harrod. *Sacred and Herbal Healing Beers: The Secrets of Ancient Fermentation*. Boulder, Colo.: Siris Books, 1998.

Byock, Jesse, transl. *The Saga of the Volsungs*. London: Penguin, 1999.

Capasso, Luigi. "5300 Years Ago, the Ice Man Used Natural Laxatives and Antibiotics." *The Lancet*, vol. 352 (1998), p. 1864.

Chardonnens, László Sandór. *Anglo-Saxon Prognostics, 900-1100: Study and Texts*. Leiden: Brill, 2007.

Christensen, Arne Emil. "Oseberg." Philip Pulsiano and Kristen Wolf, eds. *Medieval Scandinavia: An Encyclopedia*. New York: Taylor and Francis, 1993. pp. 457-459.

Cilliers, Louise. "Vindicianus's *Gynaecia*: Text and Translation of the Codex Monacensis (Clm 4622)." *Journal of Medieval Latin*, vol. 15 (2005), pp. 153-236.

Cleasby, Richard and Gudbrand Vigfusson. *An Icelandic–English Dictionary*. Oxford: Clarendon Press, 1874.

Cockayne, Oswald. *Leechdoms, Wortcunning, and Starcraft of Early England*. 3 vols. London: Longman, Green, Longman, Roberts, and Green, 1864-1866.

Davidson, Hilda Roderick Ellis. *Roles of the Northern Goddess*. London: Routledge, 1998.

Dowden, Ken. *European Paganism: The Realities of Cult from Antiquity to the Middle Ages*. London: Routledge, 2000.

Drew, Katherine Fischer, transl. *The Lombard Laws.* Philadelphia: University of Pennsylvania Press, 1973.

DuBois, Thomas A. *Nordic Religions in the Viking Age.* Philadelphia: University of Pennsylvania Press, 1999.

Eadie, M. J. "The Antiepileptic Materia Medica of Pediacus Dioscorides." *Journal of Clinical Neuroscience*, vol. 11, no. 7 (2004), pp. 697-701.

Eggen, Mette. "The Plants Used in a Viking Age Garden A.D. 800-1050." Dagfinn Moe, James H. Dickson, and Per Magnus Jørgensen, eds. *Garden History: Garden Plants, Species, Forms, and Varieties form Pompeii to 1800.* PACT vol. 42. Rixensart: Council of Europe, Division of Scientific Cooperation / PACT Belgium, 1994. pp. 45-46.

Elburg, Rengert. "A Neolithic Treasure Chest." *The European Archaeologist*, no. 33 (2010), pp. 4-6. http://www.e-a-a.org/TEA33.pdf

Etkin, Nina L. "Ethnopharmacology: Biobehavioral Approaches in the Anthropological Study of Indigenous Medicines." *Annual Review of Anthropology*, vol. 17 (1988), pp. 23-42.

Finnur Jónsson, ed. *Hauksbók.* København [Copenhagen]: Thieles Bogtrykkeri, 1892-1896.

Flateyjarbók. 3 vols. Christiana: P. T. Malling, 1862-1864.

Flint, Valerie. *The Rise of Magic in Early Medieval Europe.* Princeton, N.J.: Princeton University Press, 1991.

Flora of Iceland. http://www.floraislands.is/engflora.htm

Flower, Barbara, and Elisabeth Rosenbaum. *The Roman Cookery Book: A Critical Translation of* The Art of Cooking *by Apicius.* London: George G. Harrap, 1958.

Forbes, Thomas R. "Medical Lore in the Bestiaries." *Medical History*, vol.

12, no. 3 (1968), pp. 245-253.

Fosså, Ove. "Angelica: From Norvegian Mountains to the English Trifle." Richard Hosking, ed. *Wild Food – Proceedings of the Oxford Symposium on Food and Cookery 2004.* Totnes: Prospect Books, 2006. pp. 131-142.

Fry, Timothy, ed. *RB 1980: the Rule of St. Benedict in Latin and English with Notes.* Collegeville, Minn.: Liturgical Press, 1982.

Glander, Kenneth E. "Nonhuman Primate Self-Medication with Wild Plant Foods." Nina L. Etkin, ed. *Eating on the Wild Side: The Pharmacologic, Ecologic, and Social Implications of Using Noncultigens.* pp. 227-239. Tucson: University of Arizona Press, 1994.

Gløb, P. V. *The Mound People: Danish Bronze Age Man Preserved.* Ithaca, N.Y.: Cornell University Press, 1974.

Gougaud, Louis. "La Prière Dite de Charlemagne et les Pièces Apocryphes Apparentées." *Revie d'Histoire Ecclésiastique*, vol. 20 (1924), pp. 211-238.

Gracia, Ana, Juan Luis Arsuaga, Ignacio Martinez, Carlos Lorenzo, José Miguel Carretero, José María Bermúdez de Castro, and Eudald Carbonell. "Craniosynostosis in the Middle Pleistocene Human Cranium 14 from the Sima de los Huesos, Atapuerca, Spain." *Proceedings of the National Academy of Sciences of the USA*, vol. 106, no. 16 (2009), pp. 6573-6578.

Grant, Edward. *A Source Book in Medieval Science.* Cambridge, Mass.: Harvard University Press, 1974.

Guðni Jónsson , ed. *Eddukvæði: Sæmundar-Edda.* 2 vols. Reykjavík: Íslendingasagnaútgáfan, 1949.

Guðni Jónsson and Bjarni Vilhjálmsson, eds. *Fornaldarsögur Norðurlanda.* 3 vols. Reykjavík: Bókaútgáfan Forni, 1944.

Guðrún P. Helgadóttir. "Laukagarðr." Ursula Dronke, Guðrun P. Helgadóttir, Gerd Wolfgang Weber, and Hans Bekker-Nielsen, eds. *Speculum Norroenum: Norse Studies in Memory of Gabriel Turville-Petre*. Odense: Odense University Press, 1981. pp. 171-184.

——. *Hrafns saga Sveinbjarnarsonar*. Oxford: Clarendon Press, 1987.

Hall, Alaric. *Elves in Anglo-Saxon England: Matters of Belief, Health, Gender, and Identity*. Woodbridge, Suffolk: Boydell, 2007.

Hallmundsson, May, and Hallberg Hallmundsson, transl. *Icelandic Folk and Fairy Tales*. Reykjavík: Iceland Review, 2005.

Hansson, Anne-Marie and James H. Dickson. "Plant Remains in Sediment from the Björkö Strait Outside the Black Earth at the Viking Age Town of Birka, Central Eastern Sweden." Urve Miller, Björn Ambrosiani, Helen Clarke, Tony Hackens, Anne-Marie Hannson, and Birgitta Johansson (eds), *Environment and Vikings with Special Reference to Birka*. Birka Studies 4/PACT 52. Rixensart: Conseil de l'Europe, 1997. pp. 205-216.

Harild, Jan Andreas, David Earle Robinson, and Jesper Huldebusch. "New Analyses of Grauballe Man's Gut Contents." Pauline Asingh and Niels Lynnerup, eds. *Grauballe Man: An Iron Age Bog Body Revisited*. Moesgard: Jutland Archaeological Museum and Moesgard Museum, 2007, pp. 154-187.

Heimdahl, Jens. "Barbariska Trädgårdsmästare: Nya Perspektiv på Hortikulturen i Sverige fram til 1200-talets Slut." *Fornvännen*, vol. 105 (2011), pp. 265-280.

Heizmann, Wilhelm. *Wörterbuch der Pflanzennamen im Altwestnordischen*. Berlin: de Gruyter, 1993.

Hellmund, Monika. The Neolithic records of *Onopordum acanthium*, *Agrostemma githago*, *Adonis* cf. *aestivalis* and *Claviceps purpurea* in Sachsen-Anhalt, Germany. *Vegetation History and Archaeobotany*, vol. 17, supplement 1 (2008), pp. S123-S130.

Henry, Amanda G., Alison S. Brooks, and Dolores R. Piperno. "Microfossils in Calculus Demonstrate Consumption of Plants and Cooked Foods in Neanderthal Diets (Shanidar II, Iraq; Spy I and II, Belgium." *Proceedings of the National Academy of Sciences of the USA*, vol. 108 (2011), pp. 486-491.

Herodotus; transl. A. D. Godley. *Histories.* Vol. 2; Books III-IV. Loeb Classical Library. Cambridge, Mass.: Harvard University Press, 1921.

Hippocrates; transl. W. H. S. Jones. *Hippocrates. Vol. II.* Loeb Classical Library. Cambridge, Mass.: Harvard University Press, 1959.

—; transl. Paul Potter. *Hippocrates. Vol. IX.* Loeb Classical Library. Cambridge, Mass.: Harvard University Press, 2010.

Hortsman, C. *Yorkshire Writers: Richard Rolle of Hampole, an English Father of the Church, and his Followers.* London: Swan Sonnenschein & Co., 1895.

Hughes, Shaun. "On the Circulation of Vernacular Medical Texts in Late Medieval and Early Modern Iceland" . *New Directions in Medieval Scandinavian Studies: 30th Annual Conference of the Center for Medieval Studies.* http://www.fordham.edu/mvst/conference10/scandinavia/hughespaper.html

Huld, Martin E. "Meillet's Northwest Indo-European Revisited." Karlene Jones-Bley and Martin E. Huld, eds. *The Indo-Europeanization of Northern Europe. Journal of Indo-European Studies, Monograph no 17,* pp. 109-125. Washington, DC: Institute for the Study of Man, 1996.

Isidore of Seville; Stephen A. Barney, W. J. Lewis, J. A. Beach, and Oliver Berghof, transl. *The* Etymologies *of Isidore of Seville.* Cambridge: Cambridge University Press, 2006.

Jessen, Knud. "Planterester Fran den Ældre Jernalder i Thy." *Botanisk*

Tidsskrift, vol. 42 (1933), pp. 257-88.

Jón Árnason. *Íslenzkar Þjóðsögur og Æfintýri*. Leipzig: J. C. Hinrichs, 1862.

Jón Steffensen. "Aspects of Life in Iceland in the Heathen Period." *Saga-Book*, vol. 17 (1966-69), pp. 177-205

Julius Caesar; transl. H. J. Edwards. *The Gallic War*. Loeb Classical Library. Cambridge, Mass.: Harvard University Press, 1917.

Kaplan, Reid W. "The Sacred Mushroom in Scandinavia." *Man*, New Series, vol. 10, no. 1 (1975), pp. 72-79.

Kålund, Kr. "Den Islandske Lægebog: Codex Arnamagnæanus 434a, 12mo." *Det Kongelige Danske Videnskabernes Selskabs Skrifter, Historisk og Filosofisk Afdeling*, vol. 7 (1907), pp. 355-400.

—. *Alfræði Íslenzk: Islandsk Encyklopædisk Litteratur*. Vol. 1. Copenhagen: S. L. Møller, 1908.

Kenward, H. K. and Hall, A. R. *Biological Evidence from Anglo-Scandinavian Deposits at 16-22 Coppergate*. York: Council for British Archaeology, 1995.

Konráð Gíslason. *Sýnisbók Íslenzkrar Tungu og Íslenzkra Bókmennta í Fornöld*. Copenhagen: Gyldendaal, 1860.

Langslow, D. R. "Etymology and History: For a Study of 'Medical Language' in Indo-European." J. H. W. Penney (ed.), *Indo-European Perspectives: Studies in Honour of Anna Morpurgo Davies*. pp. 30-47. Oxford: Oxford University Press, 2004.

Larsen, Hennig. "MS Royal Irish Academy 23 D 43." *Modern Philology*, vol. 23, no. 4 (1926), pp. 385-392.

—. "The Vocabulary of the Old Icelandic Medical MS: Royal Irish Academy 23 D 43". *Journal of English and Germanic Philology*, vol. 26, no. 2 (1927), pp. 174-197.

—. *An Old Icelandic Medical Miscellany: MS Royal Irish Academy 23 D 43, with Supplement from MS Trinity College (Dublin) L-2-27*. Oslo: Det Norske Videnskaps-Akademi i Oslo, J. Dybwad, 1931.

Larson, Laurence M. *The King's Mirror (Speculum Regale—Konungs Skuggsjá)*. New York: American-Scandinavian Foundation, 1917.

Larsson, Inger and Kjell Lundquist. "Icelandic Medieval Monastic Sites—Vegetation and Flora, Cultural Plants and Relict Plants, Contemporary Plant-Names." Factsheet 2010:18, Department of Landscape Architecture, Sveriges Lantbruksuniversitet, 2010. http://pub.epsilon.slu.se/5110/1/larsson_e_al_100823.pdf

Lempiäinen, Terttu. "Macrofossil Finds of Henbane (*Hyoscyamus niger*) in the Old Settlement Layers in Southern Finland." *Review of Palaeobotany and Palynology*, vol. 73 (1992), pp. 227-239.

Lewis-Williams, J. D. and T. A. Dowson. "The Signs of All Times: Entoptic Phenomena in Upper Palaeolithic Art." *Current Anthropology*, vol. 29, no. 2 (1988), pp. 201-245.

Lincoln, Bruce. *Myth, Cosmos, and Society: Indo-European Themes of Creation and Destruction*. Cambridge, Mass.: Harvard University Press, 1986.

Lindberg, David C. *The Beginnings of Western Science: The European Scientific Tradition in Philosophical, Religious, and Institutional Context, Prehistory to A.D. 1450*. 2nd ed. Chicago: University of Chicago Press, 2008.

Lindow, John. *Norse Mythology: A Guide to the Gods, Heroes, Rituals, and Beliefs*. Oxford: Oxford University Press, 2001.

Liuzza, Roy Michael. "Anglo-Saxon Prognostics in Context: A Survey and Handlist of Manuscripts." *Anglo-Saxon England*, vol. 30 (2001), pp. 181-230.

—. *Anglo-Saxon Prognostics: An Edition and Translation of Texts from London,*

British Library MS Cotton Tiberius A.III. Cambridge: DS Brewer, 2011.

Livarda, Alexandra. "Spicing Up Life in Northwestern Europe: Exotic Food Plant Imports in the Roman and Medieval World." *Vegetation History and Archaeobotany*, vol. 20 (2011), pp. 143-164.

Livarda, Alexandra, and Marijke van der Veen. "Social Access and Dispersal of Condiments in North-West Europe from the Roman to the Medieval Period." *Vegetation History and Archaeobotany*, vol. 17, supplement 1 (2008), pp. S201-S209.

Long, Deborah J., Paula Milburn, M. Jane Bunting, Richard Tipping and Timothy G. Holden. "Black Henbane (*Hyoscyamus niger*L.) in the Scottish Neolithic: A Re-evaluation of Palynological Findings from Grooved Ware Pottery at Balfarg Riding School and Henge, Fife." *Journal of Archaeological Science* vol. 26 (1999), pp. 45-52.

Magnús Rafnsson, ed. *Tvær Galdraskræður / Two Icelandic Books of Magic*. Hólmavík, Strandir: Galdrasýning á Ströndum / Icelandic Sorcery and Witchcraft, 2008.

Majno, Guido. *The Healing Hand: Man and Wound in the Ancient World*. Cambridge, Mass.: Harvard University Press, 1975.

Mallory, J. P. and D. Q. Adams, eds. *Encyclopedia of Indo-European Culture*. Chicago: Fitzroy Dearborn, 1997.

Matthías Viðar Sæmundsson. *Galdrar á Íslandi: Íslensk Galdrabók*. Reykjavík: Almenna Bókafélagið, 1992.

Mitchell, Stephen A. *Witchcraft and Magic in the Nordic Middle Ages*. Philadelphia: University of Pennsylvania Press, 2011.

Migne, J. P. *Patrologia Latina*. Paris: Imprimerie Catholique, 1844-5.

Monumenta Germaniae Historica. Capitularia Regum Francorum. Vol. 1.

Hanover: Hahn, 1883.

Monumenta Germaniae Historica. Poetarum Latinorum Medii Aevi. Vol. 2. Berolini [Berlin]: Weidmann, 1884.

Nelson, Max. *The Barbarian's Beverage: A History of Beer in Ancient Europe.* Abingdon: Routledge, 2005.

Nordland, Odd. *Brewing and Beer Traditions in Norway: The Social Anthropological Background of the Brewing Industry.* Oslo: Universitetsforlaget, 1969.

O'Connor, Ralph, transl. *Icelandic Histories and Romances.* Stroud: Tempus, 2006.

Ólafur Daviðsson. "Isländische Zauberzeichen und Zauberbücher." *Zeitschrift des Vereins för Volkskunde,* pp. 150-167.

Opsomer-Halleux, Carmélia. "The Medieval Garden and its Role in Medicine." MacDougall, Elisabeth B., ed. *Medieval Gardens.* Washington D.C.: Dumbarton Oaks, 1986. pp. 93-114.

Pálsson, Hermann, and Paul Edwards, transl. *Seven Viking Romances.* London: Penguin, 1985.

Paxton, Frederick S. "*Signa Mortifera:* Death and Prognostication in Early Medieval Monastic Medicine." *Bulletin of the History of Medicine,* vol. 67, no. 4 (1993), pp. -650.

Pliny the Elder; H. Rackham, transl. *Natural History.* Vol. IX, Books XXXII-XXXV. Loeb Classical Library. Cambridge, Mass.: Harvard University Press, 1952.

—; D. E. Eichholz, transl. *Natural History.* Vol. X, Books XXXVI-XXXVII. Loeb Classical Library. Cambridge, Mass.: Harvard University Press, 1962.

Pollington, Stephen. *Leechcraft: Early English Charms, Plantlore, and Healing.*

Hockwold-cum-Wilton: Anglo-Saxon Books, 2001.

Polomé, Edgar C. "Who Are The Germanic People?" Susan Nacev Skomal and Edgar C. Polomé, eds. *Proto-Indo-European: The Archaeology of a Linguistic Problem. Studies in Honor of Marija Gimbutas.* Washington, D.C.: Institute for the Study of Man, 1987. pp. 216-244.

Price, Lorna. *The Plan of St. Gall in Brief.* Berkeley: University of California Press, 1982.

Reichborn-Kjennerud, Ingjald. "The School of Salerno and Surgery in the North During the Saga Age." *Annals of Medical History*, vol. 9 (1937), pp. 321-337.

Renfrew, Jane M. *Palæoethnonobotany: The Prehistoric Food Plants of the Near East and Europe.* New York: Columbia University Press, 1973.

Robertson, David. "Magical Medicine in Viking-Age Scandinavia." *Medical History*, vol. 20, no. 3 (1976), pp. 317-322.

—. "Attitudes Toward Nutrition and Health in the Ancient North." *Southern Medical Journal*, vol. 71, no. 12 (1978), pp.

Robinson, David Earle. "Plants and Vikings: Everyday Life in Viking Age Denmark." *Botanical Journal of Scotland*, vol. 46, no. 4 (1994), pp. 542-551.

Rösch, Manfred. "New Aspects of Agriculture and Diet of the Early Medieval Period in Central Europe: Waterlogged Plant Material from Sites in South-Western Germany." *Vegetation History and Archaeobotany*, vol. 17 Supplement (2008), pp. S225-S238.

Rose, Valentino. *Theodori Prisciani Euporiston Libri III.* Lipsiae [Leipzig]: B. G. Teubner, 1894.

RUNDATA 2.5: Scandinavian Runic-text Database. University of Uppsala,

2008. http://www.nordiska.uu.se/forskn/samnord.htm

Saxo Grammaticus; ed. Hilda Ellis Davidson, transl. Peter Fisher. *The History of the Danes: Books I–IX.* Woodbridge, Suffolk: D. S. Brewer, 1996.

Scully, Terence. "A Cook's Therapeutic Use of Garden Herbs." Peter Dendle and Alain Touwaide, eds. *Health and Healing from the Medieval Gardens.* Woodbridge: Boydell, 2008. pp. 60-71

Skinner, Charles M. *Myths and Legends of Flowers, Trees, Fruits, and Plants: In All Ages and All Climes.* Philadelphia: J. B. Lippincott, 1911.

Smith, William, and Samuel Cheetham. *A Dictionary of Christian Antiquities.* Hartford: J. B. Burr, 1880.

Snorri Sturluson (Lee M. Hollander, transl.) *Heimskringla: History of the Kings of Norway.* Austin: University of Texas Press, 1964.

— (Anthony Faulkes, transl.) *Edda.* London: J. M. Dent, 1987.

Solecki, Ralph S. "Shanidar IV, a Neanderthal Flower Burial in Northern Iraq." *Science,* vol. 190 (1975), pp. 880-881.

Sommer, Jeffrey. "The Shanidar IV 'Flower Burial': A Reevaluation of Neanderthal Burial Ritual." *Cambridge Archaeological Journal,* vol. 9, no. 1 (1999), pp. 127-137.

Stannard, Jerry. "Alimentary and Medicinal Uses of Plants." MacDougall, Elisabeth B., ed. *Medieval Gardens.* Washington D.C.: Dumbarton Oaks, 1986. pp. 69-92.

Stein, Ragnar. "Neurology in the Nordic Sagas". In Rose, Frank Clifford, *Neurology of the Arts: Painting, Music, Literature.* London: Imperial College Press, 2004, pp. 389-400.

Steinunn Kristjánsdóttir. "Skriðuklaustur Monastery: Medical Centre of Medieval East Iceland?" *Acta Archaeologica,* vol. 79 (2008), pp.

208-215.

Storms, G. *Anglo-Saxon Magic.* New York: Gordon Press, 1974.

Ström, Folke. *Níð, Ergi, and Old Norse Moral Attitudes.* London: Viking Society for Northern Research, 1974.

Svenska Akademiens Ordbok, http://g3.spraakdata.gu.se/saob/

Tacitus; H. Mattingly, transl., S. A. Handford, rev. *The Agricola and the Germania.* Harmondsworth: Penguin, 1970.

Thorleifur Einarsson. "Pollen-Analytical Studies on the Vegetation and Climate History of Iceland in Late and Post-Glacial Times." Áskell Löve and Doris Löve, eds. *North Atlantic Biota and their History.* pp. 355-365. New York: Macmillan, 1963.

Thorndike, Lynn. *A History of Magic and Experimental Science. Volume I.* New York: Columbia University Press, 1923.

Viðar Hreinsson, ed. *Complete Sagas of Icelanders.* Reykjavik: Leifur Eiriksson, 1997.

Voigts, Linda E. "Anglo-Saxon Plant Remedies and the Anglo-Saxons." *Isis,* vol. 70, no. 2 (1979), pp. 250-268.

Waggoner, Ben, transl. *The Sagas of Ragnar Lodbrok.* New Haven, Conn.: Troth Publications, 2009.

—. *Sagas of Fridthjof the Bold.* New Haven, Conn.: Troth Publications, 2010.

—. *Sagas of Giants and Heroes.* New Haven, Conn.: Troth Publications, 2010.

Wallis, Faith. *Medieval Medicine: A Reader.* Toronto: University of Toronto Press, 2010.

Watkins, Calvert. *How to Kill a Dragon: Aspects of Indo-European Poetics*. Oxford: Oxford University Press, 1995.

Werlauff, Eric. *Symbolae ad Geographiam Medii Ævii ex Monumentis Islandicis*. Hauniæ [Copenhagen]: Gyldendal, 1821.

White, T. H. *The Book of Beasts*. New York: G. P. Putnam's Sons, 1954.

Wilson, D. Gay. "Plant Remains from the Graveny Boat and the Early History of *Humulus lupulus* L. in W. Europe." *New Phytologist*, vol 75, no. 3 (1975), pp. 627-648.

Zohary, Daniel, and Maria Hopf. *Domestication of Plants in the Old World*. 3rd ed. Oxford: Oxford University Press, 2000.

Zysk, Kenneth G. "Reflections on an Indo-European Healing Tradition." *Perspectives on Indo-European Language, Culture, and Religion: Studies in Honor of Edgar C. Polomé, vol. 2. Journal of Indo-European Studies, Monograph 9*. McLean, Va.: Institute for the Study of Man, 1992. pp. 321-336.

ENDNOTES

1   Glander, "Nonhuman Primate Self-Medication", pp. 227-239.

2   Plants identified in the grave include *Achillea* (yarrow), *Centaurea* (knapweeds, cornflower), *Senecio* (groundsel), *Althaea* (marsh mallow), *Muscari* (grape hyacinth), and *Ephedra* (joint-fir). See Solecki, "Shanidar IV", pp. 880-881.

3   Sommer, "The Shanidar IV 'Flower Burial', pp. 127-137.

4   Henry et al. "Microfossils", pp. 486-491.

5   e.g. Gracia et al., "Craniosynostosis", pp. 6576-6578.

6   Lewis-Williams and Dowson, "Signs of All Times", pp. 201-217.

7   Etkin, "Ethnopharmacology", pp. 31-35.

8   For example, the claim that the Iron Age "Grauballe Man" was deliberately fed ergot fungus (*Claviceps purpurea*), which contains a compound similar to LSD, before being sacrificed. Ergot sclerotia were found in Grauballe Man's stomach, but probably as accidental contaminants of the grain he ate, and probably not in a high enough dosage to make him "trip". See Harild, "New Analyses", pp. 175-176.

9   Zohary and Hopf, *Domestication of Plants*, pp. 232-235.

10   Renfrew, *Palæoethnobotany*, p. 163.

11   Hellmund, "Neolithic Records," pp. S123-S130.

12   Zohary and Hopf, p. 233; Brombacher, "Archaeological Investigations", pp. 176-177.

13   Zohary and Hopf, p. 233.

14   Long et al., "Black Henbane", pp. 45-52.

15   Elburg, "A Neolithic Treasure Chest", pp. 5-6.

16   Capasso, "5300 Years Ago", p. 1864.

17   This is a simplification of a complex situation; for the best recent overview, see Anthony, *The Horse, The Wheel, and Language*.

18   Langslow, "Etymology and History", p. 32.

19   Asterisks in front of a PIE word or root mean that it is a

reconstruction, not known from existing languages or texts. The symbols h_1, h_2, etc. represent *laryngeals*—consonants articulated in the back of the throat. Their exact sound values are not known, and their existence is deduced mostly from indirect effects on the vowel system.

20   Langslow, pp. 40-41.

21   Mallory, *Encyclopedia of Indo-European Culture*, pp. 17-19.

22   Watkins, *How to Kill a Dragon*, pp. 537-539; Zysk, "Reflections", pp. 326-334.

23   Langslow, p. 42 n33.

24   Mallory, pp. 87, 351, 361-362.

25   Mallory, pp. 376-377; Watkins, pp. 523-524.

26   Lincoln, *Myth, Cosmos, and Society*, pp. 110-112.

27   Anthony, *The Horse, The Wheel, and Language*, pp. 340-370.

28   Anthony, p. 362.

29   Herodotus, *Histories*, IV.73-75; transl. Godley, pp. 272-275.

30   Huld, "Meillet's Northwest Indo-European Revisited", p. 110.

31   Pollington, *Leechcraft*, pp. 87-88; Polomé, "Who Are The Germanic People?", p. 232.

32   Gløb, *The Mound People*, pp. 51-72.

33   Gløb, *The Mound People*, p. 116

34   Pollington, *Leechcraft*, pp. 420-421.

35   Flint, *The Rise of Magic*, pp. 247-248.

36   Kaplan, "The Sacred Mushroom," pp. 72-79.

37   Nelson, *The Barbarian's Beverage*, pp. 11-12.

38   Gløb, *The Mound People*, p. 60.

39   Nordland, *Brewing and Beer Traditions*, p. 220.

40   Wilson, "Plant Remains from the Graveny Boat", pp. 644-645; Behre, "Beer Additives in Europe", pp. 39-42.

41   e.g. Buhner, *Sacred and Herbal Healing Beers*, pp. 167-175.

42   Behre, "Beer Additives in Europe", pp. 43-44.

43   Harild, pp. 158-174.

44   Harild, pp. 175-176.

45   Renfrew, *Palæoethnobotany*, pp. 179-189; Behre, "Collected Seeds", pp. 67-72; Harild, pp. 156-157.

46   *De Bello Gallico* VI:22; transl. Edwards, *The Gallic War*, p. 347.

47   *Germania* 26; transl. Mattingly, p. 123.

48   Heimdahl, "Barbariska Trädgårdsmästare", pp. 265-280; Jessen,

"Planteresten", pp. 258-259, 269-272.

49   Heimdahl, pp. 265-280.

50   Livarda and van der Veen, "Social Access", pp. S201-S209.

51   Livarda, "Spicing Up Life", pp. 143-164.

52   Apicius, *De re coquinaria*, transl. Flower and Rosenbaum, *The Roman Cookery Book*.

53   Majno, *The Healing Hand*, pp. 381-390.

54   Rösch, "New Aspects of Agriculture", pp. S225-S238.

55   MacLeod and Mees, *Runic Amulets and Magical Objects*, pp. 88-89.

56   MacLeod and Mees, pp. 21, 73-75.

57   Pollington, *Leechcraft*, p. 436.

58   *Rothair's Edict* 368, in Drew, *The Lombard Laws*, p. 125.

59   Robertson, "Magical Medicine", p. 318.

60   Dowden, *European Paganism*, p. 261.

61   Dowden, p. 65; Flint, pp. 250-251.

62   Lindberg, *The Beginnings of Western Science*, pp. 150-157.

63   Flint, *The Rise of Magic*, pp. 71-78, 254-257.

64   Flint, pp. 273-282.

65   Flint, pp. 301-309.

66   Dowden, p. 261.

67   For example, Davies, "Healing Charms", pp. 26-27, for examples from England; Bang, *Norske Hexeformularer*, nos. 1-25, pp. 1-13, for examples from Norway.

68   From Ælfric's sermon *Octabas et circumcisio Domini*; quoted in Chardonnens, *Anglo-Saxon Prognostics*, p. 117.

69   Chardonnens, pp. 126-138.

70   Flint, pp. 301-302.

71   Lindberg, pp. 320-327; for an example of the arguments made in favor of monastic medicine, see the extract from the *Lorscher Arzneibuch* in Wallis, pp. 84-93.

72   *Regulae Sancti Benedicti* 36:1-10; ed. Fry, *RB 1980*, p. 236.

73   *Regulae Sancti Benedicti* 66:6-7; ed. Fry, p. 289.

74   Price, *The Plan of St. Gall*, pp. 32-37.

75   Price, pp. 66-69.

76   Stannard, "Alimentary and Medicinal Uses of Plants", p. 74.

77   Opsomer-Halleux, "The Garden's Role in Medicine", pp. 106-112.

78   *Monumenta Germaniae Historica, Poetarum Latinorum Medii Aevi*, vol.

2, pp. 335-350; for partial translation, see Wallis, pp. 98-109.

79   Opsomer-Halleux, pp. 104-105; Voigts, "Anglo-Saxon Plant Remedies", pp. 259-260; for sources see Wallis, *Medieval Medicine*, pp. 110-116.

80   Opsomer-Halleux, pp. 104-105; Voigts, pp. 260-261.

81   *Monumenta Germaniae Historica, Capitularia Regum Francorum* vol. 1, pp. 90-91.

82   Opsomer-Halleux, pp. 98, 106-112.

83   Wallis, pp. 112-113.

84   Lindberg, pp. 329-330.

85   Lindberg, pp. 329-334.

86   Werlauff, *Symbolae*, p. 25.

87   Lindberg, pp. 330-331.

88   See note 104 below; also DuBois, *Nordic Religions*, pp. 98-100.

89   Snorri Sturlusson, *Magnúss saga ins Góða* ch. 28, transl. Hollander, *Heimskringla*, pp. 562-563.

90   He may or may not have visited Salerno itself, but he had ample opportunity to learn Salernitan medicine at the pilgrimage sites that he did visit. See Reichborn-Kjennerud, "School of Salerno", pp. 328-331; Guðrún P. Helgadóttir, *Hrafns saga*, pp. xci-cviii, 3-6; Stien, pp. 395-398.

91   Reichborn-Kjennerud, "School of Salerno," pp. 321-328.

92   Robinson, "Attitudes Toward Nutrition and Health," p. 1564; DuBois, pp. 98-99.

93   Kenward and Hall, *Biological Evidence*, pp. 525-526, 758-760.

94   Kenward and Hall, pp. 692, 752-756.

95   Robinson, "Plants and Vikings", pp. 545-548.

96   Lempiäinen, "Macrofossil Finds", pp. 227-239.

97   Barrett, "Plant and Animal Remains," pp. 41-46.

98   Christensen, "Oseberg", p. 459.

99   Hansson and Dickson, "Plant Remains", pp. 208-214.

100   Aalto and Heinäjoki-Majander, "Archaeobotany of Staraja Ladoga", pp. 24-27.

101   Åsen, "Plants of Possible Monastic Origin", pp. 229-236.

102   Einarson, "Pollen-Analytical Studies," pp. 362-363.

103   Steffensen, "Aspects of Life," pp. 193-194. Healing stones are mentioned in the Icelandic law code *Grágas*, and as late as 1550, the church at Hólar owned a stone "to ease childbirth", while

a number of Icelandic burials contained special stones that may have been considered healing or protective. See Robertson, "Magical Medicine," p. 322.

104 Ellis-Davidson, *Roles of the Northern Goddess*, pp. 161-163. Examples of women healers in the sagas include Álfgerðr in *Droplaugarsonar saga* (ch. 11, *Complete Sagas of Icelanders* vol. 4, pp. 370-371), Hildigunnr in *Njála saga* (ch. 57, *CSI* vol. 3, p. 69), and Helga jarlsdóttir in *Harðar saga og Hólmverja* (ch. 25, *CSI* vol. 2, p. 221), as well as the unnamed healer in *Fóstbrœðra saga* (ch. 24, *CSI* vol. 2, pp. 393-395, 401-402).

105 Snorri Sturluson, *Edda*, "Gylfaginning" ch. 35; transl. Faulkes, p. 29.

106 Lindow, *Norse Mythology*, p. 105.

107 Saxo Grammaticus, *History of the Danes* III.80, transl. Davidson and Fisher, pp. 77-78; IX.304, transl. Davidson and Fisher, p. 283.

108 *Lacnunga* 79-82, transl. Pollington, pp. 214-219.

109 All quotations from the *Poetic Edda* are from the text of Guðni Jónsson, *Eddukvæði*; the translations are mine.

110 Stien, "Neurology in the Nordic Sagas", pp. 392-393. Note that the Old English *Lacnunga* also prescribes earthworms for inflamed or infected skin (ch. 99, transl. Pollington, p. 223).

111 "Mailcoat-assembly" is a kenning for battle; a "tree of battle" is a warrior, i.e. one who stands firm and upright like a tree in the midst of the fighting.

112 MacLeod and Mees, *Runic Amulets and Magical Objects*, pp. 25-27.

113 MacLeod and Mees, pp. 118-119.

114 MacLeod and Mees, pp. 120-121. "He fucked the sorceror" need not be taken literally; it implies the utter defeat and humiliation of the one who sent the fever, whether a human enchanter or a spirit.

115 MacLeod and Mees, pp. 123-129.

116 MacLeod and Mees, pp. 34-35.

117 MacLeod and Mees, pp. 132-133.

118 *Laxdæla saga* ch. 60; *Complete Sagas of Icelanders*, vol. 5, p. 92.

119 Guðrún Helgadóttir, "Laukagarðr", pp. 178-179.

120 ch. 13; *Complete Sagas of Icelanders*, vol. II, pp. 360-361.

121 Snorri Sturluson, *Óláfs saga Tryggvasonar* ch. 92, transl. Hollander, *Heimskringla*, p. 226.

122 Fosså, "Angelica", pp. 132-133; see also Eggen, "Plants Used in a

Viking Age Garden", pp. 45-46.

123 ch. 12; *Complete Sagas of Icelanders*, vol. I, p. 200.

124 *Fóstbræðra saga* ch. 24, *Complete Sagas of Icelanders* vol. 2, pp. 393-395, 399-402; Snorri Sturluson, *Óláfs saga helga* ch. 234, transl. Hollander, *Heinskringla*, pp. 519-520.

125 Guðni Jónsson and Bjarni Vilhjálmsson, *Fornaldarsögur Norðurlanda* vol. I, p. 91; transl. Waggoner, *Sagas of Ragnar Lodbrok*, p. 2.

126 *Fornaldarsögur Norðurlanda*, vol. I, p. 18; transl. Byock, *Saga of the Volsungs*, p. 45.

127 *Fornaldarsögur Norðurlanda*, vol. 3, pp. 337-340; transl. Waggoner, *Sagas of Giants and Heroes*, pp. 99, 101-102. See Appendix 2.

128 e.g. *Þorsteins saga Víkingssonar, Fornaldarsögur Norðurlanda*, vol. 2, p. 45; transl. Waggoner, *Sagas of Fridthjof the* Bold, pp. 9-11; *Mírmanns saga*, transl. O'Connor, *Icelandic Histories and Romances*, pp. 264-265.

129 Snorri Sturluson, *Ynglinga saga* ch. 4, transl. Hollander, *Heinskringla*, p. 8.

130 *Völsa þáttr*, in *Flateyjarbók*, vol. 2, p. 363.

131 *Egils saga einhenda, Fornaldarsögur Norðurlanda*, vol. 3, p. 180; transl. Pálsson and Edwards, *Seven Viking Romances*, p. 250.

132 *Göngu-Hrólfs saga, Fornaldarsögur Norðurlanda* vol. 2, p. 415; transl. Pálsson and Edwards, *Göngu-Hrolf's Saga*, p. 82.

133 Larson, *King's Mirror*, ch. 10.

134 Guðrún Helgadóttir, "Laukagarðr", pp. 178-9

135 Larsson and Lundquist, "Icelandic Medieval Monastic Sites".

136 Guðrún Helgadóttir, "Laukagarðr", p. 175.

137 Larsen, *Medical Miscellany*, p. 154; Guðrún Helgadóttir, "Laukagarðr", p. 184. *Baldurs-brá* can refer to several species in the genera *Matricaria* and *Anthemis*, but is perhaps most likely to be sea-chamomile, *Matricaria maritima*; see Heizmann, p. 93.

138 Steinunn Kristjánsdóttir. "Skriðuklaustur Monastery", pp. 208-215.

139 Larsen, *Medical Miscellany*, pp. 21-23.

140 As suggested by Hughes, "Old Norse Vernacular Texts".

141 Larsen, *Medical Miscellany*, pp. 24-25.

142 Larsen, "MS", p. 387.

143 Hughes, "Circulation of Texts".

144 Kålund, *Den Islandske Lægebog*, p. 395.

145 *Lacnunga* 37; transl. Pollington, *Leechcraft*, p. 197.

146 *Lacnunga* 31, transl. Pollington, p. 195.

147 Larsen, "MS", pp. 387-388.

148 Hughes, "Circulation of Vernacular Medical Texts"

149 DuBois, p. 97.

150 See Jón Árnason, *Íslenzkar Þjóðsögur og Æfintýri*, vol. 1, pp. 484-606; for a selection of tales in English translation, see Hallmundsson and Hallmundsson, *Icelandic Folk and Fairy Tales*, pp. 59-68.

151 Ólafur Davíðsson, "Isländische Zauberzeichen und Zauberbücher," p. 151.

152 Flowers, *Galdrabók*, pp. 13-20.

153 Magnús Rafnsson, pp. 14-20.

154 http://gandalf.uib.no:8008/corpus/menota.xml.

155 The text reads *óbláta*, "offering," which in Church usage means the sacramental bread baked for the Mass, usually before it has been formally consecrated and become *hostia*, the Host. (Smith, *Dictionary of Christian Antiquities*, vol. 2, p. 1418.) This and the next several remedies all seem to involve writing on sacramental bread. There are parallels in Anglo-Saxon texts; the well-known charm *Against a Dwarf* (*Wið Dweorh*) involves writing seven saints' names on seven *oblata* and hanging them around the afflicted person's neck (*Lacnunga* 93, transl. Pollington, *Leechcraft*. pp. 220-221; see also Storms, *Anglo-Saxon Magic*, no. 36, pp. 276-277).

156 *Enn-ducas* could be *inducas*, "you lead", in Latin, possibly derived from *et ne nos inducas in tentationem*, "And lead us not into temptation", in the Lord's Prayer. The other words are obscure; *kérion* is Greek for "honeycomb", and *bion* and *agrion* could be forms of the words for "life" and "wild; savage; undomesticated," but why these words should be used here is not clear.

157 Writing a word repeatedly, progressively lengthening it or truncating it by one letter each time, is known from other medical charms (e.g. Storms, *Anglo-Saxon Magic*, p. 153; MacLeod and Mees, pp. 138-139). In one version recorded from Norway, the patient eats a slip of paper with a magic word on it; each day, the word is decreased by one letter, presumably making the illness decrease by sympathetic magic (Kvideland and Sehmsdorf, *Scandinavian Folk Belief*, 28.11, pp. 138-139). The aim here may be that the patient's strength and health should increase as the length of the magic words increases. The words themselves are seemingly meaningless.

158   The magic words are gibberish. MS Royal Irish Academy 23
       D 43 uses similar words in blood-stopping charms: *fres* † *prares*
       † *res* † *pax* † *vax* † *nax* † (Larsen, *Medical Miscellany*, p. 138) and
       fres pres res rereres reprehex (Larsen, *Medical Miscellany*, p. 139). A
       blood-stopping charm in AM 461 has *pax, vax, vax, hero, boro, iuva*
       tartar gegimata, and another in the same manuscript has *sumax pax*
       (Kålund, *Alfræði Íslenzk*, vol. 3, pp. 109, 111).

159   *ridu* could also mean "chills and fever", depending on whether
       the *i* is long or short. I have translated it "riding", i.e. being ridden
       or possessed by trolls or witches, because of the context in which
       it appears. The magic words are gibberish, but their increasing
       length may be intended to increase the sufferer's vigor; see note
       157 above.

160   A garbling of *Tetragrammaton, Alpha et Omega. Tetragrammaton*, "Four
       Letters" in Greek, refers to the true name of God, represented
       by four Hebrew letters, *yod he vav he* or *YHVH. Alpha et Omega*,
       the first and last letters of the Greek alphabet, make up another
       title for God, i.e. "First and Last" or "Beginning and End". This
       formula appears in a Norwegian rune inscription (N248) dated
       to 1270-1315 (RUNDATA 2.5), and in a 16th-century Icelandic
       grimoire (Flowers, *Galdrabók*, no. 42, p. 54) The formula is
       often abbreviated *alpha et o+*, which may be responsible for the
       misreading *alpha edol.*

161   The text reads *alfa-volkun*, a hapax legomenon; the *Dictionary of Old*
       Norse Prose suggests that it might refer to rickets. The concept of
       elves or alfar as malevolent beings who cause illness is widespread;
       see Hall, *Elves in Anglo-Saxon England*, chs. 4-5.

162   The Latin reads "In the name of the Father and Son and Holy
       Spirit", with three names inserted. Allowing for some creative
       spelling, Samuel, Misael, and Raguel may be three of the Seven
       Archangels listed in the extra-biblical Book of Enoch (Saraqael,
       Michael, and Raguel); in any case, the *-el* ending is typical of angelic
       names. It may have seemed fitting to counter elves by invoking
       angels.

163   This is so ungrammatical that an exact translation is impossible.

164   A garbled version of the palindromic formula *Sator arepo tenet*
       opera rotas, which appears in full later in the manuscript. See note
       261.

165   As in note 162, three names have been inserted into "In the name of the Father and Son and Holy Spirit". The same charm appears in AM 461 (Kålund, *Alfræði Íslenzk*, vol. 3, p. 112), in which *Sinnisael* is replaced by *Missael*. These are the Hebrew names of the three young men cast into the fiery furnace by Nebuchadnezzar (Daniel ch. 3): Hananiah, Mishael, and Azariah—better known by their Babylonian names: Shadrach, Meshach, and Abednego. Having survived the flames, they would naturally be invoked to help with skin inflammations. These three men are invoked in several rune amulets and charms against burning pain (MacLeod and Mees, pp. 157-159).

166   Garbled, although the first two words could be *funderet peccatorum*, "he poured out [his blood] for sinners".

167   The first words of this charm are untranslatable, although they resemble other magic words in this and other manuscripts (see note 158 above). *Prodiui* means "I have gone". *Esto labia volunnt* is hard to parse; the best I can do is "May it be! The lips desire." *Post hoc dormivit* means "after this he has slept" (possible error for *dormibit*, "he will sleep"); it may not be part of the charm itself, but a description of what should happen, mistakenly grouped with the charm words. The same charm appears in AM 461 (Kålund, *Alfræði Íslenzk*, vol. 3, p. 111-112).

168   Except for *ne-amon*, these are names of the Hebrew letters *vav*, *nun*, *daleth*, *aleph*, *gimel*, and *ayin*. The meaning is unclear, although it's possible that the first four letters are meant to spell a title of God, *Adon* or *Adonai* (aleph-daleth-vav-nun). "*Ne-amon*" might be the Hebrew word for "faithful" (*ne'eman*).

169   The name given in the manuscript, *astimaca*, could also refer to the carrot (*Daucus carota*), a close relative of the parsnip (*Pastinaca sativa*). Classical writers did not distinguish between parsnips and carrots (Zohary and Hopf, p. 203). "Mura" is related to German *Möhre* and Swedish *morot*, meaning carrots.

170   This verse is in the complex *dróttkvætt* form in the original; I've made no attempt to duplicate the rhyme and meter. Kålund (p. 12) notes that the word "hear" (*heyra*) in line 6 is "odd", although it fits the meter perfectly. Versions of the same bloodstopping charm appear in MS 23 D 43 (Larsen, *Medical Miscellany*, pp. 139) and in later Icelandic folklore (Kvideland and Sehmsdorf, *Scandinavian*

Folk Belief, 28.6, pp. 135-136).

171   This is a hodgepodge of Latin phrases. *Libera me domini* is "Free me, Lord" (assuming a mistaken *domini* for *domine*), found in the Requiem Mass liturgy. *Sanguinis lixta* could be a mistake for *sanguinis fluxus*, "a flow of blood"; the phrase is used to describe the ailment of a woman who is healed by touching Jesus's robe (Luke 8: 43-48). Alternatively, the whole phrase could derive from Psalm 50:16, *libera me de sanguinibus Deus*, "deliver me from blood [i.e. the guilt of bloodshed], God." *Sanguinis unda* means "flood of blood". By comparison with similar phrases in MS 23 D 43, the sense of *sct sit stetid iordanis plum qdus in iordanis baptizatus* is "as the Jordan River stopped when [Jesus was] baptized in the Jordan" (Larsen, *Medical Miscellany*, p. 52). *Consummatum est*, "It is finished", are among the last words of Jesus on the cross; they appear twice in the blood-stopping charms in MS 23 D 43 (Larsen, *Medical Miscellany*, pp. 50, 53), once in a blood-stopping charm in AM 461 (Kålund, *Alfræði Íslenzk*, vol. 3, p. 111), and in a charm against nosebleeds in the 16th-century *Galdrabók* (Flowers, no. 4, p. 41). Since these phrases all deal with flows of blood or other fluids, it would be natural to use them in blood-stopping charms. References to Jesus stopping the Jordan River are common in blood-stopping charms from later Scandinavian folklore (e.g. Bang, *Norske Hexeformularer*, nos. 1242-1251, pp. 548-555; Larssen, *Medical Miscellany*, pp. 24-25; Kvideland and Sehmsdorf, *Scandinavian Folk Belief*, 28.5, p. 135) and in later British folklore (Davies, "Healing Charms", pp. 20-21).

172   Short for *In nomine patris et filii et spiritus sancti*, "In the name of the Father and Son and Holy Spirit."

173   A parallel text appears in several Anglo-Saxon manuscripts (MS Cotton Caligula A. xv. fol. 127a; Cockayne, *Leechdoms*, vol. 3, pp. 154-155) and in two Norse manuscripts (*Hauksbók*, p. 469; GKS 1812 4to, in Kålund, *Alfræði Íslenzk* vol. 3, p. 73). A Latin version is (very doubtfully) attributed to Bede (Migné, *Patriologia Latina*, vol. 90, p. 960). However, in these texts, it is men born on these three days, not conceived, whose bodies will not decay.

174   St. Birgit's Day is February 1 (assuming that St. Birgit of Kildare is meant here); St. Paul's Day could be January 25 (the Feast of the Conversion) or February 10 (the Feast of St. Paul's Shipwreck).

St. Agatha's Day is February 5. The Old English texts put one of these fateful days in late December and the others in early January, but the version in *Patrologia Latina* places them on the VI kalends, III kalends, and ides of February (January 26, January 29, and February 13), much closer to the dates in AM 434a.

175 "St. Mary's Day during the fast" is probably the Feast of the Annunciation, March 25. The Feast of *St. Peter ad Vincula* (St. Peter in Chains) is August 1, commemorating Peter's miraculous release from captivity; the author may have confused it with the Feast of Sts. Peter and Paul, June 29. St. Sylvester's Day is December 31.

176 These three days on which it is dangerous to let blood are known as the *dies egyptiaci*, "Egyptian Days", in Old English texts. Fourteen versions of this text in Latin and Old English are known from English manuscripts (Liuzza, "Anglo-Saxon Prognostics", p. 185). At least one of them, the *Lacnunga* (189, transl. Pollington, pp. 244-245) closely parallels AM 434a, with a few differences of detail; for example, eating goose is fatal within 40 days in *Lacnunga*, not 120 days as in AM 434a. The English texts identify these days as the last Monday in March, the first Monday in August, and the last Monday in December, rather than referring to saints' feast days.

177 The identity of "Aronkur" is unknown. It might even be a misspelling of "Arcanum", used for Hippocrates's legendary manuscript, hidden in his tomb (see note 193; Larsen, *Medical Miscellany*, p. 47).

178 Many medieval texts list unlucky days or "Egyptian days" for bloodletting, but few seem to list good days for it. The source here may be a short treatise attributed to Bede (probably wrongly), *De Minutione Sanguinis* (Migné, vol. 90, p. 960), which mentions that the best days for bloodletting fall between VIII Kalends of April to VII Kalends of June (March 24 through May 25). A parallel text in AM 194 ("Blóðlát", in Kålund, *Alfræði Íslenzk*, vol. 1, pp. 83-84) is nearly identical to AM 434a but calls for bloodletting on March 6, April 11, and six days from the end of May.

179 The runes read "Olafr. Olafr. Haralldr. Haralldr. Eirikr" in a late version of the rune alphabet (the complete alphabet used appears at the very end of the manuscript). These are probably intended to be the names of kings, possibly St. Olaf Haraldsson of Norway,

Harald Gormsson of Denmark, and St. Eric IX of Sweden, all renowned as Christianizers of their nations. Jón Árnason mentions a very similar charm for winning at backgammon; see Appendix 2.

180 A fragment of Psalm 129, known as *De profundis* or "Out of the depths". The complete Latin (verse 4) reads *quia apud te propitiatio est: et propter legem tuam sustinui te Domine*, "for with you there is forgiveness, and because of your law, I persevered with you, Lord."

181 "In the name of the Lord, Amen." This charm has many parallels in Icelandic grimoires (charms 33 and 45, in Flowers, *Galdrabók*, pp. 51, 55; charms 1, 2, 6 in Magnús Rafnsson, *Tvær Galdraskræður*, pp. 26-31; also see Appendix 2).

182 Possibly the Icelandic saint Jón Hólabiskup (feast days March 3 and April 23), but a similar charm in the 16th century *Galdrabók* (no. 45, in Flowers, p. 55) calls for the action to be done on St. John's Eve, June 23, a day close to the summer solstice and known in folklore all over Europe as a day for strange goings-on.

183 The Latin means something like "Who created you, who [did something] to the thief or the raging one by means of you".

184 Several later Icelandic books of magic contain spells or charms that require the writing down of strings of letter-like signs of unclear meaning. Kålund's edition turns most of these signs into ordinary letters of the Latin alphabet, but in later *galdrabókar* they are written in a stylized fashion and are often not clearly identifiable as Latin letters at all. In some cases they are clearly late variants of the rune alphabet (Flowers, *Galdrabók*, spells 13-15, 17-19, pp. 43-44); in other cases they more resemble cursive Roman letters (Jón Árnason, vol. 1, p. 464; Lbs 2413 8vo, charm 47, 58, in Magnús Rafnsson, *Tvær Galdraskræður*, pp. 63, 71; Óláfur Davíðsson, "Isländische Zauberzeichen und Zauberbücher," p. 273). Anglo-Saxon spells also call for writing strings of letters or signs (e.g. Storms, *Anglo-Saxon Magic*, nos. 32, 33, 44, pp. 268-271, 282). Several inscribed amulets also contain "nonsense" strings of rune letters, which may be encodings of charm words. Examples include the Lindholmen amulet from Denmark which includes the sequence **aaaaaaaazzznnnbmuttt**, and bracteates with inscriptions like **llet oz.rïïlï.aþzmtl**; see MacLeod and Mees, pp.

72-73, 90-93.

185 Uterine vellum (*carta virginea*) is made from the skin of unborn or stillborn animals. Kålund (*Lægebog*, pp. 14-15) notes that it has a long history of magical use.

186 Three equal-armed crosses with the arms ending in circles are used in a charm against a human enemy in the Icelandic grimoire Lbs 2413 8vo from ca. 1800 (Lbs 2413 8vo, charm 82; in Rafnsson, *Tvær Galdrasakræður*, pp. 86-87). Such crosses turn up in other spells in the same grimoire to neutralize enmity and hatred (charms 95, pp. 94-95; charm 103, pp. 100-101)

187 The original word is abbreviated, and the meaning is unclear; the editors of AM 434a reconstructed it as *herbrad*. It might be *herbráð*, "war-suddenness", i.e. "sudden attack"; *herbragð*, "stratagem"; or, as Kålund suggested (*Lægebog*, p. 45), *herboð*, "summons to war."

188 An *ophan* (literally "wheel") is a type of angel in the Jewish angelic hierarchy. *AGLA* is a Hebrew acronym signifying God; it stands for *attah gibor le'olam adonai*, "thou art strong to eternity, Lord." *AGLA* is fairly common on medieval amulets from Scandinavia; see MacLeod and Mees, pp. 134-135, 143-145, etc., for examples.

189 The above prayer is almost identical to one found in a 17th-century Icelandic grimoire (Flowers, *Galdrabók*, no. 26, p. 48). The first two full lines were recorded by Jón Árnason; one is supposed to recite them while wearing the *Ægishjálmr* or "Helm of Awe" on the brow. See Appendix 2.

190 The verb *þversýna* is a hapax legomenon (*Dictionary of Old Norse Prose*). I have assumed that it's a calque on Latin *trans-figuro*.

191 *Fjölnir* is a name of Odin in Eddic and skaldic poetry, as well as the name of a mythical king descended from the god Freyr. The name may mean "the All-Knowing". (Lindow, *Norse Mythology*, p. 116)

192 These are verses of a hymn to the Virgin Mary known as the Akathist or Acathistus. The "official" version reads: *Ave per quam gaudium splendebit. Ave per quam maledictio deficiet. Ave cadentis Adam resurrectio. Ave lacrimarum Evae redemptio. Ave altitudo inascensibilis humani cogitationibus. Ave profunditas invisibilis et angelorum oculis. Ave quae es imperatoris solium. Ave quae portas portantem omnia. Ave stella demonstrans solem. Ave uterus divinae incarnationis. Ave per quam renovatur creatura.* "Hail to you through whom joy will break forth.

81

Hail to you through whom the curse will end. Hail, resurrection of fallen Adam. Hail, redemption of Eve's tears. Hail, height inaccessible to human reason. Hail, depth unseen even by angels' eyes. Hail, you who are the king's throne. Hail, you who bear the one who bears everything. Hail, star who reveals the sun. Hail, womb of the divine incarnation. Hail, you through whom creation is renewed."

193 From the story about Ypocras (Hippocrates) to the end of the monthly calendar, AM 434a parallels the text known as *Læknisfræði* in AM 194, although the section on prognostics is truncated in AM 434a (Kålund, *Alfræði Íslenzk*, vol. 1, pp. 61-64). The story about Hippocrates hiding his books in his tomb goes back to a 5th- or 6th-century text called *Capsula eburnea* ("Ivory Casket", referring to a casket that Hippocrates supposedly kept his books in; see Paxton, "Signa Mortifera", pp. 639-640; Wallis, p. 43). *Capsula eburnea* was widely copied, and the story appears in AM 194 and MS 23 D 43, and also turns up in medieval Irish and German texts (Larsen, *Medical Miscellany*, p. 47).

194 These prognostics do resemble some of those found in the Hippocratic corpus, such as *Prognostic* (chapters II-VI); the description of the sick man's face, the well-known *facies Hippocratica*, seems particularly close (II.5-11, transl. Jones, p. 9). A few seem garbled; *Prognostic* claims that sweating only on the head is a bad sign, while sweating all over the body can be good (VI.8-11, transl. Jones, p. 15; see also *Prorrhetic I* no. 39, transl. Potter, p. 181). A more direct source is probably one of the pseudo-Galenic texts which circulated widely in the Middle Ages, some of which were distantly derived from Hippocratic texts; see Wallis, pp. 43-45.

195 The original, *mal bledu vaz*, is unclear (Kålund, *Lægebog*, p. 16).

196 This list of recommendations for each month of the year is a *regimen*. Often attributed to Hippocrates, regimens were common in continental Europe—over fifty have been identified—and varied a great deal. While I have not compared the AM 434a regimen with all others, it closely resembles the Latin regimen in an English manuscript (BL Harley 3271), although AM 434a is more terse (Chardonnens, *Anglo-Saxon Prognostics*, pp. 471-475).

197 *by af dufu unga*; the parallel in MS 23 D 43 has *dufna saur*, "dove's excrement" (Larssen, *Medical Miscellany*, pp. 120, 204).

198 The word is *atar-mata*, a borrowing of Latin *atramentum*, which could mean any dark liquid, but usually ink or dye.

199 This remedy and two others in this book prescribe the gall of an eel for eye troubles. The source may be the apocryphal Book of Tobit in the Bible (6:8, 11:1-13), in which Tobias cures his father Tobit's blindness with the gall of a giant fish. A rune inscription from Bergen, Norway, dated to 1335, as well as several written Scandinavian charms for healing the eyes, refer to this story (MacLeod and Mees, pp. 157-158).

200 AM 434a just reads *Vid allz konur*, "against all kinds". The parallel passage in AM 194 specifies that this remedy is against all kinds of *eitri*, "poison; venom".

201 AM 434a reads *hleif surann*, "sour loaf." The parallel in AM 194 reads *hleif þurran*, "dry loaf".

202 The "swallow stone" or *lapis cheliodonus* as a cure for epilepsy goes back at least to the Greek herbalist Dioscorides, and was still being prescribed as late as 1675. In most versions of this remedy, there are two stones of different colors in a swallow's stomach; sometimes both are to be used together, while in other texts only one is effective. See Eadie, "The Antiepileptic Materia Medica", p. 698.

203 AM 434a reads *baunu*, which could mean "beans", albeit ungrammatically. But a duplicate of this prescription in AM 434a has *bunu*, and other manuscripts have *búu* or *bunu*, which is mugwort (*Artemisia vulgaris*); see Kålund, *Lægebog*, p. 24.

204 The text is corrupt here; I've tried to make the best sense of it that I can. The sentence about coughing illnesses was probably introduced from a completely different source. (Kålund, *Lægebog*, pp. 20-21)

205 The original has *ymprez*, which doesn't seem to make sense. AM 194 has *yfiz* (presumably the subjunctive of normalized *ýfast*), which would literally mean "to be ruffled" but could also mean "to be ripped."

206 *Calamitatis* might be *cadmea* or *calamine*, an old name for zinc-containing minerals. Pliny (*Natural History* XXXIV.xxii.100-105; transl. Rackham, pp. 200-205) described very similar recipes for making salves by roasting *cadmea*, quenching it in wine, and then sifting it through cloth.

207   According to Heizmann (p. 92), "ambrosia" could refer to a number of fragrant plants, such as yarrow (*Achillea millefolium*) and species of *Artemisia* (mugwort, wormwood, etc.) Opsomer-Halleux ("The Garden's Role in Medicine", p. 106) suggests that ambrosia is in fact wormseed (*Chenopodium botrys*).

208   The word translated "unmanliness" is *ergi*, one of the worst insults that could be flung at a man. *Ergi* applied to a man can connote passive homosexuality, but it does not necessarily have a sexual meaning, and can simply mean cowardice or failure to defend one's honor. (Ström, *Old Norse Moral Attitudes*, pp. 17-20) Its association with "all lusts" suggests that it might refer to homosexual desires here.

209   "He" is the man whose urine is used in this test. This prognostic appears in a Danish leechbook from the 1300s, AM 187 (Mitchell, *Witchcraft and Magic*, p. 47).

210   See notes 225-226 for a discussion of wearing peony as a treatment for epilepsy.

211   Or possibly "as small as a snake", depending on whether the word *litt* is read with a short or a long *i*. But the text has already referred to the herb *dragunncia*, an arum, as being spotted like a snake; presumably this is the herb meant here.

212   The Old English *Lacnunga* (112; transl. Pollington, pp. 224-225) prescribes deer antler ash in wine for tears.

213   This remedy turns up in a 12th-century Latin bestiary (White, *A Book of Beasts*, p. 39), but apparently not in other bestiaries (Forbes, "Medical Lore", p. 248).

214   "Unmanliness" is *ergi* again; here it isn't clear whether the word has sexual connotations or not. See note 208 above.

215   The manuscript reads *burðar-dyrr*, "birth-door".

216   *Solsequium* means "sun-follower" in Latin, but its identity is unclear. Heizmann suggests that it could be pot marigold [*Calendula officinalis*], chicory [*Cichorium intybus*], or dandelion [*Taraxacum* sp.]. Opsomer-Halleux ("The Garden's Role in Medicine," p. 111) suggests that medieval *solsequia* is probably chicory.

217   A partial parallel to this recipe appears in the Old English *Bald's Leechbook*, which recommends sulfur (possibly; the text is unclear) and ink, along with burned salt, for a spot on the eye. (transl. Pollington, pp. 382-383)

218   The original is unclear: *siod i vatnni III kiot-vellur*, "boil in water three meat-boilings". My translation is tentative; see note 234.

219   AM 655 XXX begins here.

220   The original says to give the man *súrur* (literally, "sour things") to eat. In medical texts, *súrur* can mean sorrel or dock (*Rumex* sp.); houseleeks (*Sempervivum tectorum*), or sour bread dough. Heizmann (p. 128) suggests that "sorrel" is the likeliest meaning here.

221   The *Old English Herbarium* also recommends smearing ground rue on the forehead as a headache remedy. (91.6, transl. Pollington, p. 331)

222   *Flugormr*, "flying snake", seems strange, but the Old English *Nine Herbs Charm* mentions *attor. . . fleogan*, "venom [that] flies" (line 55; also Pollington, *Leechcraft*, p. 217). The *flugormr* may be a metaphor for some sort of airborne infection.

223   Greek and Roman medical authorities recommended earth with a seal on it, *terra sigillata* (Stein, p. 391). But also see *Hávamál* 137: *hvars þú öl drekkir, / kjós þér jarðar megin, / því at jörð tekr við ölðri*—"when you drink ale, / choose earth's might, / because earth counters a drinking bout", as well as the Old English charm *eorþe þe on bere ealle hire mihtum ond magenum,* "May Earth bear you up with all her powers and might" (*Bald's Leechbook* 63, transl. Pollington, p. 405)

224   Presumably coral, although possibly red jasper; Pliny (*Natural History* XXXVII.lvi.153; transl. Eichholz, pp. 288-289) mentions a red stone called *corallus*, but does not ascribe any medicinal benefits to it.

225   Dioscorides (ca. 40-90 AD) wrote *De Materia Medica*, a large and influential compendium of medical knowledge, especially medicinal plants. His work was widely copied and used throughout the Middle Ages. Dioscorides described peony, but did not actually claim that it staved off epilepsy; see Eadie, "The Antiepileptic Materia Medica", pp. 697-699.

226   Galen, or Claudius Galenus (129-200 AD), was an influential Roman physician and philosopher. His extensive medical writings formed the core of medical teaching in medieval Europe. He did observe that a peony root hung around a boy's neck seemed to stave off epilepsy, while removal of the root caused seizures. (Thorndike, *History of Magic*, p. 173) Peony was still being prescribed to be worn to ward off seizures as late as 1675 (Eadie,

"The Antiepileptic Materia Medica", p. 700)

227   The *Old English Herbarium* also recommends celandine against dimming sight (75.1-2, transl. Pollington, p. 321).

228   AM 434a reads *upxa gall.* AM 655 reads *ufsa gall*, "gall of the pollock fish" (*ufsi*). But Harpestræng's work reads *oxæ*, and Macer's Latin original has *bovino* (Kålund, *Lægebog*, p. 29).

229   AM 434a and AM 655 XXX both read *þat er vex aa vidi*—"what grows on a willow" [*viðir*]. Evidently, a word dropped out; MS 23 D 43 has *ber þat er vex á viði*—"berry that grows on a willow", probably a willow catkin. (Larsen, *Medical Miscellany*, p. 110; Heizmann, *Wörterbuch*, p. 131)

230   The *Old English Herbarium* also recommends fennel against bladder ailments, albeit in a somewhat more elaborate preparation (126.2, transl. Pollington, p. 345).

231   AM 655 ends here.

232   The original reads *lungna veislu*, which would literally be "feast of the lungs"; this is presumably an error for *veilsa*, "pus" (Larsen, p. 195).

233   *Pater Noster* = "Our Father", the Lord's Prayer; *Credo in Deum* = "I believe in God", the Creed.

234   The original is unclear: *siod III kiot-vellr i vatnni*, "boil three meat-boilings in water". The parallels in other texts aren't any clearer; MS 23 D 43 has *siod þat i vatni þriar kiot vellur*, "boil it in the water of three meat-boilings". Larsen (p. 186) tentatively interprets *kjöt-vella* as "meat broth". My translation is also tentative.

235   Translation conjectural; the text reads *spolorm*, normalized to *spólormr*, literally "spool-worm". In another manuscript *spólormr* substitutes for *skorpion*. (*Dictionary of Old Norse Prose*).

236   Literally "a green wound" (*græn sar*); *grænn* can mean "fresh", but this could also mean a literally green wound, presumably an infected one.

237   Ambergris is secreted and regurgitated by sperm whales. It was long used in perfumery.

238   This section contains several references to remedies or humans being hot or cold, moist or dry. This is classical Greek medical theory: the four elements (earth, air, water, fire), and in parallel with them the four humours that determined a person's physiological nature (blood, phlegm, yellow bile, black bile), were described

using pairs of four opposing qualities. Air and blood are hot and moist; water and phlegm are cold and moist; fire and yellow bile are hot and dry; and earth and black bile are cold and dry. Disease was caused by an imbalance in the body's humours, and the goal of treatment was to bring them back into balance. Foods and drugs were chosen because their qualities were those that the patient was lacking. See Lindberg, p. 336-338; Scully, "A Cook's Therapeutic Use of Garden Herbs", pp. 60-65.

239   Possible reference to hemorrhoids?

240   The text reads *kolnnaa kuldaa*, meaning something like "chilling cold", but this is probably a mistake; Harpestræng's text reads *bolnæ koddæ*, "swollen scrotum" (Kålund, *Lægebog*, p. 34)

241   Medicines were classified not only according to their qualities (hot/cold, moist/dry; see note 238 above), but by their degrees of each quality.

242   The original reads *lannga sott briosti*, but *lannga* may be a mistake for *lunga*; Harpestræng's corresponding text reads *saar a lungæ oc i bryst*, "sore (or wound) on the lungs and in the breast".

243   The original *of sic* is hard to understand. *Sic* implies something sinking down or being let down slowly (cf. Old Norse *síga*, "to sink down", *sig*, "a rope that is let down"). Kålund (*Lægebog*, p. 36) points out that other Icelandic authors list *sig* as a term for a protruding anus; *of* would be a prefix meaning "excessive". I've translated *of sic* as "prolapsed rectum", but it's also possible that the author meant *ufsig*, "prolapsed uvula". (Larsen, "Vocabulary", p. 194)

244   The word here is *pyckviz* (normalized infinitive *pykkvast*), which according to the current *Dictionary of Old Norse Prose* is a hapax legomenon. Assuming it is related to the adjective *pykkr*, it would mean something like "he becomes thick", possibly "he becomes strong"; Larsen (*Medical Miscellany*, p. 213) translated the parallel passage in MS 23 D 43 in this way. But *pykkr* can also mean a blow or hit (cognate with English *thwack*). Russian and Finnish steam baths both involve light beating or whisking with birch branches. I conjecture that the steam bath that the author had in mind also involved whisking, and that this is the word for it.

245   Both steam baths and water baths, including medicinal baths, appear in various Icelandic sagas; see DuBois, pp. 100-101.

246   The ultimate source of this embryology text is not "Ysodorus" (Isidore of Seville); while he does discuss human embryology in his *Etymologiae*, his text is not very close to AM 434a (XI.i.143-145, transl. Barney et al., pp. 240-241). Rather, the source may be the late Roman author Helvius Vindicianus, whose *Gynaecia* (ca. 400) includes a month-by-month description of fetal development that includes a number of the same "milestones" as AM 434a. Isidore incorporated facts from the *Gynaecia* into his *Etymologiae*, and later copyists inserted material from *Etymologiae* into the *Gynaecia* (Cilliers, "Vindicianus's *Gynaecia*", pp. 158-159); the AM 434a passage may go back to such a hybrid text.

247   The paragraph up to this point is closely parallelled in a short text called *Myndan mannslíkama* in AM 194 (Kålund, *Alfræði Íslenzk*, vol. 1, pp. 55-56)

248   AM 434a is not especially close to the clearest recension of the *Gynaecia*, the 12th-century Codex Monacensis (Cilliers, ch. 21, pp. 180-183). It more closely resembles some of the earlier versions (e.g. Codex Parisinus 4883, and St. Gall. 751; ed. Rose, *Theodori Prisciani Euporiston* pp. 452-456). However, the timing and order of events in most recensions of *Gynaecia* differs from that in AM 434a: The mother feels sick in month 3 or 4, not 6; the fetus begins to resemble its parents in month 5, not 7; and the bones harden in month 8, not month 3. Vindicianus also does not mention the arrival of the soul (Cilliers, p 224). An Old English text that also describes embryology by month (T14 in Liuzza, *Anglo-Saxon Prognostics*, pp. 200-201), does mention that a fetus "comes alive" and gains a soul in the fifth month, but the text otherwise differs in detail from both the *Gynaecia* and AM 434a; the relationship between T14 and the *Gynaecia* is not clear (see discussion in Liuzza, *Anglo-Saxon Prognostics*, pp. 57-58). What may be the closest parallel to the AM 434a text is a paragraph clearly derived from the *Gynaecia*, incorporated in the writings of Trotula of Salerno (ch. 12; Grant, *Source Book in Medieval Science*, p. 765); the order of events is much closer to that of AM 434a, although AM 434a appears to have shifted forward by one month.

249   The above is not marked as poetry in the original text, but most of its lines alliterate according to Eddic meters, albeit not always perfectly. A parallel turns up in the *Flateyjarbók* version of

Fóstbræðra saga: "A man's anger resides in his gall, his life-blood in his heart, his memory in his brains, his ambition in his lungs, his laughter in his spleen and his desire in his liver." (ch. 21; transl. in *Complete Sagas of Icelanders*, vol. 2, p. 374)

250 This sentence is probably garbled; the parallel passage in AM 461 reads "These men, says Ysidorus, have a cold nature." (Kålund, *Alfræði Íslenzk*, vol. 3, p. 110) Ysidorus is Isidore of Seville; this section of AM 434a only loosely resembles his explanation of infertility (*Etymologiae* XI.i.142, transl. Barney et al., p. 240). A passage by Trotula of Salerno (transl. in Grant, p. 764) is somewhat closer, discussing excesses of heat, moisture, and cold in both men and women.

251 The Sator square, *sator arepo tenet opera rotas* (meaning something like "The sower Arepo uses wheels in his work") is a well-known square palindrome; when written in a 5x5 square of letters, it reads the same, horizontally or vertically, in either direction. Dating at least to the first century CE, it was widely copied and thought to be magically potent; it appears on at least three runestones from Sweden (RUNDATA 2.5), on several other artifacts from Scandinavia, and in Icelandic books of magic (e.g. Lbs 2413 8vo; ed. Rafnsson, p. 109; Flowers, *Galdrabók*, pp. 19-20, 32-33; Ólafur Davíðsson, "Isländische Zauberzeichen und Zauberbücher," pp. 161-163; see also Appendix 2).

252 The first four words are hard to parse, although Machumetus is a version of the name Mohammed. The remainder reads "by the holy virginity of Mary who brought Jesus Christ from her womb by the word of the archangel Gabriel." I have not been able to trace these words to a Biblical or liturgical source.

253 This spell appears in AM 431 12mo, prefaced with the title *lausn ifir iodsiukre konu*, "release over a woman in childbirth". (Kålund, *Alfræði Íslenzk*, vol. 3, p. 86)

254 The manuscript has *heilla* here, which would mean "enchants, bewitches, spellbinds". The word is rarely used in a positive sense. While this is possible, I've assumed that *heila*, "makes whole", is what is meant here.

255 This prayer is taken from one of the many legendary "letters from heaven" that were popular in the Middle Ages. In one version of this legend, an angel brought a letter to Pope Leo, who gave it to

Charlemagne before he went out to battle at Roncesvalles. The contents of the letter vary a great deal, but they usually include a version of the prayer quoted here, the "Prayer of Charlemagne". Mentioned in 13th-century texts, the prayer was often said to protect the one who read it, heard it, or carried it against weapons, fire, drowning, and enemies. Texts of the prayer vary, but usually include crosses interspersed with the words of an invocation to the Cross of Jesus Christ. (Gougaud, "La Prière Dite de Charlemagne", pp. 227-238). Daviðsson ("Isländische Zauberseichen", p. 164 n2) quotes a version of this prayer from a mid-19th century Icelandic manuscript, which he translates into German; a 15th-century version, in Latin, appears in Hortsman (*Yorkshire Writers*, p. 376). Kålund (*Lægebog*, p. 37) notes that the text is in an odd "Danish-colored" language, riddled with grammatical errors.

256   This is a *lunarium*, a list of prognostications based on the day of the lunar cycle. Kålund notes that AM 194 has a Latin lunarium (*Prognostica*, in Kålund, *Alfrœði Íslenzk*, vol. 1, pp. 84-89); *Hauksbók* includes another, unfortunately not well preserved (p. 469, *Pronostica temporum*), while AM 435 includes a lunarium in Norse (Kålund, *Alfrœði Íslenzk*, vol. 3, pp. 105-108). These all vary in details, but an 18th-century Norse manuscript (AM 245) has a much closer parallel text to AM 434a. Lunaria begin appearing in manuscripts in the 9th century, and are well-known from English and continental manuscripts. Specialized lunaria predict dreams coming true, the advisability of letting blood or taking other actions, the fate of those who get sick, or the fates of children born; general lunaria cover most or all of these (Liuzza, *Anglo-Saxon Prognostics*, pp. 21-38). Lunaria are quite variable, and tracing the textual history of the AM 434a lunarium is beyond the scope of this book. I will only note that the most complete general lunarium from England (MS Cott. Tiberius A iii. fol. 30b, in Latin with Old English glosses) has a number of details in common with the AM 434a lunarium at the beginning (except for the birth prognostics), but the details diverge about midway through. (Liuzza, text T2, pp. 124-147)

257   A literal translation of *tungu-skært*; but Old English parallels suggest that this could be an error for *tungu-skætt*, "evil-tongued".

258   Following Kålund (p. 39) in reading *ofsa áhyggju* for the original *of þana hyggiu faa*.

259 Assuming that *mana* is a mistake for *manna*; if *mána* is meant, this would mean "judgment of the moon".

260 *skelmis-drep*, literally "blow from a demon", means an epidemic or livestock plague (Cleasby and Vigfusson, p. 543).

261 *purra-verkr* literally means "dry pain"; it survives in Swedish as *torrvärk*, meaning pain or inflammation of the joints, including gout, rheumatism, and so on. (*Svenska Akademiens Ordbok*, "Torrvärk")

262 The source of "Galienus's" signs is a pseudo-Galenic text called *Signa Mortifera*, which was widely circulated; see Paxton, p. 649; Wallis, p. 45.

263 This is a rune alphabet, with a number of letters that were not part of the older rune futharks. The letters spell **a b c d e f g h i k l m n o p q r s t u x y æ z þ.**

264 *Skáldskaparmál* 18, transl. Faulkes, p. 82.

265 This is in western Iceland, in Dalasýsla county, south of the Westfjords (*Vestfirðir*) peninsula.

266 This story is told in ch. 6 of *Geirmunds þáttr heljarskins* in the compilation *Sturlunga saga*. A handy translation is available at http://www.oe.eclipse.co.uk/nom/Geirmund.htm .

267 In July 1627, Barbary pirates from Algiers raided eastern Iceland and the Westman Islands, carrying off prisoners to be sold into slavery. The raids are known in Icelandic history as *Tyrkjaránið*, "the Turkish Abductions." (Algeria was under Ottoman Turkish rule at the time.)

268 Rowans will often sprout new shoots from the roots if the main trunk is cut down.

269 A long fjord in northern Iceland; the present-day city of Akureyri is on the Eyafjord. *Möðrufellshraun* is a lava flow south of the head of the Eyafjord.

270 On the other hand, Skinner (pp. 55-56) cites a Norwegian folk belief that a rowan plank should be used in every ship, because "Thor would take care of his own."

271 One ell is about two feet (61 cm), but the exact length varied in different places and times. Assuming that Jón Árnason meant the Danish ell (24.7 inches, 62.77 cm), these trees would stand between 12.4 and 16.5 feet tall (3.8–5 meters). By Icelandic standards, these are very tall trees. Eggert Ólafsson wrote an account of his travels in Iceland between 1752 and 1757.

272 Located in the Westfjords peninsula in northwest Iceland.

273 The story appears in *Grettis saga*; a sorcerous woman carves runes on a stump, which washes up on the island where Grettir and his friends are living. When Grettir tries to chop up the stump for firewood, his axe turns in his hands and cuts into his leg; despite bandaging, the wound becomes infected and leaves him incapacitated when his enemies come after him. (chs. 79-82, *Complete Sagas of Icelanders*, vol. 2, pp. 170-176)

274 Jón Árnason describes how the "sea-mouse" (*flæðarmús*) is to be caught and used to attract money, also using a stolen coin. In modern Icelandic, *flæðarmús* refers to a marine segmented worm (*Aphrodite aculeata*), but the beast that Jón Árnason describes is probably mythical. (*Íslenzkar Þjóðsögur og Æfintýri*, vol. 1, pp. 429-430)

275 The mandrake is not native to Iceland; the directions for harvesting it are essentially identical with the widespread medieval legend. However, the mandrake's ability to attract coins resembles the Icelandic legend of *nábrókar* ("necropants" or "corpse breeches"). "Necropants" are made from skin flayed whole from the lower half of a dead body, and worn like trousers over the sorceror's own skin. When a coin stolen from a poor widow is placed in the necropants' scrotum, it will draw more coins. (Jón Árnason, *Íslenzkar Þjóðsögur og Æfintýri*, vol. 1, pp. 428-429)

276 The Icelandic names are *lasagrás* and *fjögra laufa smári*. *Smári* usually means "clover", and several species of true clover are native to Iceland. However, Dr. Maurer, another early folklore researcher and one of Árnason's sources, identifies this plant with *Paris quadrifolia*, known in English as Herb Paris, which does have four leaves on a central stalk, but which is not otherwise very similar to clovers (it's a close relative of the trilliums). *Smári* does appear in the names of a few other non-clover plants.

277 The *Flora of Iceland* lists "Brana's herb" (*Brönugras*) as *Dactylorhiza maculata*, but "couple's herb" (*hjónagras*) as *Pseudorchis straminea*, and "Frigg's herb" (*Friggjargras*) as *Platanthera hyperborea*. These are all native orchids, and fairly easy to confuse with each other.

278 The story is told in *Hálfdanar saga Brönufóstra*; see *Fornaldarsögur Norðurlanda*, vol. 3, pp. 337-340; transl. Waggoner, *Sagas of Giants and Heroes*, pp. 99-102.

279   The *Flora of Iceland* identifies "devil's finger" (*skollafingur*) as fir clubmoss, *Huperzia selago*, and "devil's herb" (*skollagras*) as the brown seaweed *Chordaria flagelliformis*. It adds that *Blechnum spicant*, deer fern, is known as "devil's comb" (*skollakambur*).

280   An early 19th-century book of magic calls for cutting variants of this symbol on the sides of an animal if it is a victim of *gletting*, literally "pranking" or "bantering" but implying a sort of curse. (Lbs 764 8vo no. 26, in Magnús Rafnsson, *Tvær galdraskræður,* pp. 242-243)

281   Icelandic books of magic include spells that begin with these lines, but they are decidedly not love charms; they are *fretrúnir,* "fart runes", intended to make the victim suffer severe gastrointestinal distress, with lines like *skíttu nú eða springdu,* "shit now or explode!" (Flowers, *Galdrabók,* no. 46, p. 55; Lbs 2413 8vo, no. 67, in Magnús Rafnsson, *Tvær Galdraskræður,* pp. 76-77) Whether this reflects real variation in the use of this formula, or results from ignorance or bowdlerization on the part of Jón Árnarson or his sources, is not known to me.

282   An older name for the collection of poems now called the *Poetic Edda,* based on the mistaken belief that it was compiled by the Icelandic clergyman Sæmundr the Learned. The reference to the "sleep-thorn" appears in the poem *Sigrdrífumál.*

283   Presumably some sort of cipher alphabet. Substitution ciphers are used in some of the later Icelandic grimoires to write key words; e.g. Lbs 2413, in Magnús Rafnsson, *Tvær galdraskræður / Two Icelandic Books of Magic.*

284   *Buslubæn,* "Busla's Prayer", is a long poetic curse, spoken by the witch Busla in the legendary *Bósa saga ok Herrauðs.* At its end are six groups of runes that must be unscrambled. (*Fornaldarsögur Norðurlanda* vol. 2, p. 474; transl. Pálsson and Edwards, *Seven Viking Romances,* pp. 207-208). The runes are a variant of what is known as the *thistill-mistill-kistill* formula, known from several runestones and other inscriptions; see MacLeod and Mees, pp. 145-147.

285   *Jesus Christus mundum liberavit* is "Jesus Christ liberated the world"; I have not been able to decode the abbreviation *"sat. ser."*

286   In a manuscript from 1660, there are words written in the rings, one inside each ring: "JHE HOVA", "re dem tor", and "IHS CHS" in the first set of rings, "VIKA NUEI", "DOM IN US", and "DE

US" in the second set; and "SA TOR", "AR EPO", and "RO TAS" in the third. The third set of rings contains three words from the "Sator square" (see notes 164 and 261. The first and second mostly contain names or titles of God; "IHS CHS" is an abbreviation for "Iesus Christos", and "VIKA NUEI" might be a corruption of the archangel's name "Mikael". (Matthías Sæmundarsson, *Galdrar á Íslandi*, pp. 124-125)

INDEX OF PLANT NAMES

C

cabbage (*Brassica oleracea*) xix, xxiii, 7, 12, 13
caper spurge (*Euphorbia lathyris*) xxvi
caraway (*Carum carvi*) xix, xxvii, xxxiv
carrot (*Daucus carota*) xxvi, xl, 77
catmint (*Nepeta cataria*) xix, xxvi, xxvii
celandine (*Chelidonium majus*) xxvi, xxvii, 7, 13, 18, 86
celery (*Apium graveolens*) xii, xiii, xix, xx, xxiii, xxiv, xxvi, xl, 15, 16, 19
centaury (*Centaurea centaurium* or *Centaurium erythraea*) xx, xxxix, 8, 13, 17
chamomile (*Matricaria* sp.) xxviii
chard (*Beta vulgaris*) xxiii
chervil (*Anthriscus cerefolium*) xxiii, xxviii
chicory (*Cichorium intybus*) xix, xxxix, 84
    see also: "follow-the-sun"
cinnamon (*Cinnamomum verum*) xxiv, 7
clover (*Trifolium* sp.) xvi, 92
cloves (*Syzygium aromaticum*) 12
coriander (*Coriandrum sativum*) xix, xx, xxiii, xxvi, xxvii
cornflower (*Centaurea* spp.) xxvi, xxxix, 69
    see also: centaury
costmary (*Tanacetum balsamita*) xxiii
creeping thyme (*Thymus serpyllum*) 17
cress (*Lepidium sativum* or *Nasturtium officinale*) xix, xxiii, xxvii, xxviii, 9
cubeb (*Piper cubeba*) 22
cumin (*Cuminum cyminum*) xix, xxiii, xxiv, 12, 18, 19

D

dandelion (*Taraxacum* sp.) xxxix, 84
deer fern (*Blechnum spicant*) 93
dill (*Anethum graveolens*) xiii, xvi, xix, xxiii, xxiv, xxvi, 19
dittany (*Origanum dictamnus* or *Dictamnus alba*) 20
dock (*Rumex acetosa* or *R. oblongifolia*) xii, xix, xxvii, xxxviii, xxxix, 12, 15, 85
dwarf nettle (*Urtica urens*) 43
    see also: nettle

E

elder (*Sambucus nigra*) xiii, xx, xxvi, xxvii
elecampane (*Inula helenium*) 22
elm (*Ulmus* sp.) 12
emmer wheat (*Triticum dicoccum*) xviii
    see also: wheat
ergot (*Claviceps purpurea*) xiii, xviii, xxix, 69

L

lady's mantle (*Alchemilla filicaulis*) 45
laurel (*Laurus nobilis*) xxxvii, 8, 12
leek (*Allium porrum*) xx, xxiii, xxvi, xxx, xxxii, xxxiii
lemon balm (*Melissa officinalis*) xi, xii, xiii, xx
lettuce (*Lactuca* sp.) xxiii, xxxix
licorice (*Glycyrhiza glabra*) 23
lily (*Lilium candidum*) xxiii, 11
lingonberry (*Vaccinium vitis-idaea*) xix
lovage (*Levisticum officinale*) xxiii, xxiv, xxvii, 6, 19

M

madder (*Rubea tinctoria*) 17
male fern (*Dryopteris filis-max*) 7, 8, 10, 12, 13, 14
mallow (*Malva sylvestris*) 7
mandrake (*Mandragora officinarum*) 44, 92
marjoram (*Origanum vulgare*) xxvii
marsh mallow (*Althaea* sp.) 69
marsh marigold (*Caltha palustris*) 46
mastic (*Pistacia lentiscus*) xix, 7
meadow rue (*Thalictrum aquilegifolium*) 46
meadowsweet (*Filipendula ulmaria*) xvii, xxvii, 46, 52
mint (*Mentha* spp.) xxiii, xxiv, xxvii, xxxviii, 17, 18
motherwort (*Leonurus cardiaca*) xxvii
mugwort (*Artemisia vulgaris*) xxvi, xxviii, 10, 15, 83, 84
mustard (*Sinapis alba* or *Brassica nigra*) xii, xix, 23, 24
myrrh (*Commiphora* sp.) xxxviii, xxxix, 19

N

nettle (*Urtica* sp.) xxvi, xxvii, xxviii, xxxiv
        see also: dwarf nettle
night-leek (*Allium* sp.?) 16
Norwegian cud-weed (*Omalotheca norvegica*) 47

O

oak (*Quercus* sp.) xxix, 1, 43, 53
oats (*Avena sativa*) xviii
onion (*Allium cepa*) xxiii, xxiv, 14
opium (*Papaver somniferum*) 16
        see also: poppy
orchids 45, 92
oregano (*Origanum vulgare*) xix

P

parsley (*Petroselinum crispum*) xiii, xix, xxiii
parsnip (*Pastinaca sativa*) xii, xix, xxiii, xxvi, xxvii, 2, 77
pear (*Pyrus* sp.) xx
peas (*Pisum sativum*) xiii, 12
pennyroyal (*Mentha pulegium*) xxiii, xxiv, 6, 7, 8, 9, 16, 19, 20
peony (*Paeonia officinalis*) 12, 18, 85
pepper (*Piper nigrum*) xix, xxiv, xxxvii, xxxviii, 8, 10, 12, 15, 19, 23
pine (*Pinus* sp.) 23
plantain (*Plantago* sp.) xii, xix, xxvi, xxvii, xxviii, xxxiv, 13, 16, 17, 20
poppy (*Papaver somniferum*) xii, xix, xxiii, xxvi, xxvii
    see also: opium
pot marigold (*Calendula officinalis*) xxxix, 84
    see also: "follow-the-sun"
purslane (*Portulaca oleracea*) 12

R

radish (*Raphanus sativus, R. raphanistrum*) xii, xix, xxiii, 7, 9, 12, 14, 20
rhubarb (*Rheum* sp.) 6
rose (*Rosa* sp.) xiii, xxiii, xxvi, xxvii, 9
rosemary (*Rosmarinus officinalis*) xxiii
rowan (*Sorbus aucuparia*) 40, 41, 42, 43, 91
royal fern (*Osmunda regalis*) xvii
rue (*Ruta graveolens*) xix, xxiii, xxiv, 6, 7, 8, 17, 18, 20, 85
rye (*Secale cereale*) xvi, xviii, xxix, 16, 19

S

saffron (*Crocus sativus*) 22
sage (*Salvia officinalis*) xxiii, xxiv, xxxviii, 7, 9, 15
savory (*Satureja* sp.) xxiii
    see also: summer savory, winter savory
seaweed 93
sesame (*Sesamum indicum*) xix
shallots (*Allium cepa* var. *aggregatum*) xxiii
sorrel (*Rumex acetosa* or *R. acetosella*) xii, xix, xxvi, xxvii, xxxix, 10, 11, 17, 21, 85
southernwood (*Artemisia abrotanum*) 7, 9, 15
spikenard (*Nardostachys jatamansi* or *Valeriana celtica*) xix, 21
spruce (*Picea abies*) 8
summer savory (*Satureja hortensis*) xix, xxiii, xxvi, 12, 19
    see also: savory, winter savory
sweet flag (*Acorus calamus*) xxvii
sweet gale (*Myrica gale*) xvi, xvii, xxvi, 17, 23

CPSIA information can be obtained
at www.ICGtesting.com
Printed in the USA
BVHW08s0511220818
524964BV00001B/129/P

9 780578 092706